FOOD
EAT WITH EASE EVERY DAY

FOOD
EAT WITH EASE EVERY DAY

AMY FREINBERG-TRUFAS

Eat With Ease Publishing, Valatie, NY
2022

Published by *Eat With Ease Publishing*,
POB 218, Valatie, NY 12184, USA,
Website: www.amyfreinberg.com

ISBN 979-8-49756-697-0

Barbara Reina, Developmental Editor
Henrietta Sampson, Book Designer
Dan Doyle Photography, Cover Photo

 Visit my website

 Connect with the *Food: Eat with Ease Every Day Community* page on social media

Dedication

In loving memory of my grandma,
Mary Emma Hunt.
"I love you so."

In memory of my mom,
"How about some nice fruit cup?"
and dad,
"Where'd you go? What'd you eat?"

And last but not least, to Levi.
Thank you for encouraging me to tell my story.
I love you.

Contents

Disclaimer

Free and paid hardcover, paperback, kindle, audiobooks, ebooks, posts, and programs, herein referred to as "products," created by Amy Freinberg-Trufas, are based on her personal experiences, intended for educational and informative purposes only, and not intended to serve as medical or professional advice. You should consult your physician or other health care professional before making any changes to, or starting any nutritional, dietary or fitness program to determine if it is right for your unique needs.

This work is a memoir and is based upon real events. It reflects the author's present recollections of experiences over time. Some names and characteristics have been changed, some events have been compressed, and some details and dialogue have been recreated or altered for the purpose of fictionalization. Any likenesses to real people is strictly coincidental.

Amy Freinberg-Trufas spent the majority of her life living in a severely overweight body. This ultimately did not work for her, so she embarked on a journey to lose weight and regain her health. However, Amy is acutely aware that not everyone living in a larger body shares her interest, need, or desire to lose weight. By sharing her story, she in no way, shape, or form, intends to judge, advise, or shame anyone—regardless of body size, shape, or composition—into losing weight.

Foreword

Maybe you've picked up this book because you feel a little lost, wondering if there is a better road to a healthy relationship with food other than desperately summoning all of your willpower as you begrudgingly resign yourself, once again, to a lifetime of dieting, guilt, and deprivation.

Read on, and you just might see yourself in this story: times when you were abused, shamed, punished, and rewarded with food; instances when you were picked on by peers or harassed by strangers; and experiences when you felt humiliated by the very medical community you turned to for help.

Amy's story of learning to eat with ease after a lifetime of obesity is powerful and heroic. It's a brilliant and beautiful example of all the good that can come from releasing yourself from the struggle with food, and instead eating in a way that feels good to you.

I know this because I am an executive nutrition coach. In my work over the past two decades, I have had the privilege of meeting and working with the "Amys" of this world, people who, at times of deep pain and suffering, brilliantly relied on food as the solution for their emotional survival.

Yes, I said, "brilliant." Yes, I said, "solution."

There's an invitation here for you, the reader, to recognize and acknowledge, maybe for the first time, that the things that have happened to you in your childhood and in your life show up in your eating. Many of us eat for reasons that have nothing to do with sustenance, because food is a solution for more than just filling an empty belly. Food has the power to shift our emotional and physiological state. And the fact that you reached for food as a solution to a problem is not a sign that you are bad or broken, but that you are brilliant. Like Amy so bravely shares in her story, eating can move us out of pain and into (temporary) comfort. Food can help us survive difficult things at times in our lives when we had nothing else to turn to.

Amy's vulnerable and honest perspective comes from the hard times of her real-life journey. She is a voice for many who have suffered deep pain at the hands of a diet-loving, fat-shaming society, and a voice for the masses who've had their worlds shaped in homes with abuse, addiction, and emotional neglect, only surviving in the comfort and company of food.

When someone lands in trouble with food, there's history behind it. As humans, we don't intentionally choose things that make life hard for us. We pick these things because, at some point in our experience, they proved to be an adaptive solution to something we were working through. But what was once adaptive has now become maladaptive.

This was the case for Amy. Her painful yet poignant life experiences led her to the realization that overeating was not working for her anymore, and that she wasn't wrong for having eaten the way she did for the first four decades of her life. Amy brilliantly recognized that the path out of her maladaptive relationship with food was not to do more harm to herself with deprivation and punishment and struggle, but to create ease for herself and a pattern of eating motivated by love.

That was the shift.

And Amy got it right.

I've seen time and time again the power of an eating strategy built from a place of joy and ease. Being kind and gentle with yourself while eating in a way that aligns with how you want to live your life—that's the path out. The rest of the diet world will come around…eventually. Until then, we look to the "Amys" of this world to shine a light on what is possible.

Reading Amy's story, I was struck by the fact that she could have come out the other side of her difficult childhood hardened with a bitterness and mistrust in the world, but instead, Amy is here for you in these pages—openhearted and warm, with a giddy excitement at the possibility that her story might help you. My wish for you is that you lean in, allow yourself to be bathed in Amy's light, and see a hopeful path take shape in the stories and strategies she presents to you here.

Tuck your inner critic away for a short while and cozy up with this book. Let Amy's story show you how to drop the rope on the tug of war weight-loss battle once and for all. You may feel inspired to embark on your own journey of creating a life founded in love and kindness.

It's heroic work.

I'm rooting for you.

— Irene Pace, Executive Nutrition Coach, Founder of Pace Nutrition Inc., Author of *"Eat Like You Teach: How to Reset Your Weight and Reclaim Your Life"*, Host of Twitch TV's fun meal prep talk show, *"Chop Talk"*.

Acknowledgments

I would like to thank Barbara Reina, my editor and crib buddy, who skillfully guided me through the writing process and steadily encouraged me to share my truth in my voice. To Henrietta Sampson, my book designer, thank you for meticulously making my thoughts and words look beautiful. And to Fred Jones, thank you for believing in my story and for mentoring me through the process of publishing this book.

To April Walker, Pilates instructor extraordinaire, thank you for helping me find my corsets, both physical and spiritual. You're a wonderful teacher and soul sister. You're hemmed in.

To Glenn Rugen, M. Suzanne Hicks, Kelly Braswell, and Dan Grinmanis, thank you for your clinical expertise and support in my quest to understand the inner workings of my physical and emotional body as I shed 150 pounds. Your compassionate care was life-changing for me.

To Audrey Vasquez, thank you for being a bright light, and for your thoughtful insight and unwavering encouragement. I'm not sure you know how very special you are, but I certainly do.

To Joan and Thom Besch, thank you for your willingness to read a few half-finished versions of this manuscript. Your insightful feedback was instrumental in creating clarity. I look forward to many more healthy, fun dinner parties.

To my lifetime best friends Kimmy, Caren, and Robin, I love you. Growing up with each of you was my saving grace. And to Mrs. H., thank you for your gentle kindness.

To my sisters and brothers, thank you for the Sunday family dinners and fun nights playing dictionary. Sibling relationships are the longest relationships throughout our lives. I am lucky to be on this journey with each of you.

To my brother Mark, I miss you and your incredible sense of humor. Thank you for being a great big brother. Your sons are wonderful. I got them.

To the next generation of Freinbergs, I hope the stories I share in this book give you some insight and historical context. Everything can be healed. It just takes desire, time and love. I am so proud of each and every one of you. And remember: "Make the life you want. Be happy."

To Levi and Cristi, I am so fortunate to have our little family of three.

To everyone who challenged me in ways both negative and positive, thank you. I am who I am now because of you and I am grateful to you for this.

And finally, thank you to all the former Amys who bravely worked through life to get me here.

We made it.

Dear Reader,

I recently took a quiz that was designed to discover my life's passion. I thought it might be "helping others" or "writing." Guess what? It was food! I panicked! "Oh no!" I thought to myself, "I'm the same out-of-control, unhealthy food addict I've always been, and any minute now, I'm going to crumble, lose control of what I put in my mouth, and gain back 150 pounds!"

I had to stop for a moment and think about this seemingly disturbing revelation. "Wow. Food is still my passion." I really let this idea sink in. Then it dawned on me. Yes. Food is my passion. But for the first time in my life, *my passion is working for me instead of against me*. My passion for food is now serving me as I create delicious, healthy meals that I enjoy plentifully. My passion for food is what has led me right here—to want to share with you my journey, my story, my ups and downs, and my ultimate victory over the suffering and anguish I put my mind and body through during the first four decades of my life.

And my life has changed in ways I never could have imagined.

This experience has led me to reconceptualize my own value. Now, I treat myself as well as I treat anyone in my life whom I love. From time to time, I look at my own eyes in the mirror and am able to say the words, "I love you, Amy."

I hold deep concern for myself, who I am, and how I wish to stand in this body, in this world, at this moment. I actively work to honor my deepest wishes and create a life that aligns with my best dreams for myself.

I think gratefully about the miracle of the human body and its ability to heal. This fills me with awe.

I've learned that I can face problems head on, and use my creativity to solve them. I am empowered and able.

I surround myself with supportive people who feel called to help others as I do. And in this circle, I've learned that I am here to help others who were suffering as I was, with a debilitating food cycle that's keeping them stuck in a body that doesn't allow them to live the life of their dreams.

A good friend recently asked me, "With all the weight you've lost, how did you get rid of your loose skin?"

My answer: "I didn't."

When you lose a significant amount of weight, there's almost always loose skin. This happens because when you had more flesh, the skin stretched to accommodate it, like a balloon. When you lose weight and your flesh takes up less space inside your skin, the loose skin deflates and looks like a shriveled balloon.

I went to a plastic surgeon to find out what would be involved in removing the extra skin on my upper arms, which some people call "batwings." He wanted $16,000 to "fix" both of my upper arms, but advised me that instead of loose skin, I'd have large, ropey scars running down the backs of both arms.

I skipped the surgery.

I'm now at ease with my upper arms.

Know how?

I made a new choice.

I now think about that loose skin on my upper arms as the wings that helped me fly out of my former body.

And I know now why I suffered the way I did. It's led me here.

I'm here to help the person sitting at home, feeling utterly stuck and desperate for change, watching someone else's success story, and falsely believing it can never happen for them. I'm that person who has been through a life-altering experience, and now I want to extend my hand to help anyone who may be where I was—totally burdened, both emotionally and physically, with weight. I want you to know that you can move through this in a way that aligns with your deepest truth, and create a healthy life full of happiness.

The same way my father's deathbed words forever changed me, I hope to be that clarifying moment for you.

At the end of each chapter, you'll find journal prompts to help you discover your own thoughts, feelings, and emotions as they relate to creating ease in your own life. I invite you to complete them as you feel ready.

Every time you see the image of the bird throughout this book, please think about your wings.

With love,

Amy

Amy Freinberg-Trufas
Author

CHAPTER 1

___

Overweight: A Memoir of Dis-Ease

I've been overweight for as long as I can remember.

In my kindergarten photo, all I could see was my round face and broad shoulders dwarfing everyone else in my class. I was the tallest and fattest kid there and would be for my entire school life.

I had long, thick, dark brown hair that ran down my back. My mom braided it into two pigtails well over eighteen-inches long. This was our morning routine every day: my mom brushing and braiding my hair—her long fingers taming my "rat's nest" as she called it, into two long, shiny braids.

"If I don't braid your hair," she'd warn, "you'll catch head lice. You stay away from those other kids, and don't rest your head on the back of the bus seat." For safety and practicality then, this was my hairstyle every day for years. And for years, I was known for those long braids.

The first day of my summer vacation was about to begin. I was ten years old. That morning, my mom came into my room with a steely, "all business" attitude and asked, "Amy, do you know how to braid your own hair?" Wanting to please her, I quickly said, "Oh, yes, Mommy! Watch me!" and I gathered and twirled my thick hair into two deftly crafted, neat-looking braids.

"Good." She said. "You're going to fat camp."

Looking back, I still don't understand how a ten-year-old, who never left home for as much as an overnight stay at a friend's house, was suddenly, somehow ready to go away—to *fat camp* of all places—for the entire summer, just because she could braid her own hair.

The next hour or so was a blur, some sort of bad dream from which I couldn't wake up. Someone had secretly packed a trunk with clothes, a hairbrush, two bath towels, a beach towel, a huge bathing suit that was someone else's with stretched-out elastic, and some old-fashioned maxi pads and sanitary belts with safety pins in case I got my period for the first time. The trunk was old and musty and had been in the basement for years. Someone had painted it blue and inscribed my name: AMY FREINBERG in large letters across the top of it. Recognizing my sister's handwriting, I realized that I was the only one who didn't know I was going to fat camp that morning.

It was planned. Everyone in the family knew about it—except me.

In my mind, I was a freak. Even my own family didn't think I was okay as I was. Their plan was simple. Send me away and make me skinny. I wouldn't see my grandma or my best friend for the entire summer.

I went from rarely being away from home to spending an entire summer forced to be on a diet with people I didn't even know.

My parents walked me to my dad's metallic copper Cadillac, which we called "The Daddy Caddy." He told me to ride in the front passenger seat—normally a special treat and my mom's usual spot. My mom sat right behind me.

I cried and begged them not to make me go away. I promised I wouldn't eat. I promised them I would lose weight. I pleaded with them to take me back home. They said it was for my own good. For the entire three-hour ride, my mom tried to catch my attention in my side view mirror and make faces at me to make me laugh. I just cried.

Fat Camp

Fat camp was everything I was terrified it would be and more: Lots of people sleeping in bunks, one outside bathroom for everyone, open showers, and groups of girls, some slim, some chunky, already forming cliques. Even at fat camp, the pecking order was still in place. I was assigned a bed and kept my blue trunk at the foot of it.

Some kids at camp were skinny and I learned later that they were there because their families "were having big problems." By default, skinny kids were deemed the cool kids, along with all the kids from New Jersey, who were just a little overweight.

Every morning at 7:00 a.m., the camp loudspeaker woke us with a bugle playing *Reveille*. This was our call to quickly wake up, dress, and walk to the dining hall for breakfast. The menu left much to be desired. Breakfast was usually a small box of unsweetened bran cereal and a carton of slightly soured skim milk, or scrambled eggs served rubbery and cold. After breakfast, we did calisthenics. Lunch was around noon . . . a salad with vinegar or a hot dog with no bun along with baked beans and fruit from a jar, or the occasional piece of fresh fruit. Then, more calisthenics, crafts, nature walks, swimming, or jumping jacks. I did jumping jacks for hours, braids flying everywhere, slapping me in my face as I jumped for what seemed like forever. Dinner was next . . . a piece of skinless baked chicken or a plain hamburger with canned vegetables. Once in a while, we had overcooked spaghetti, served lukewarm in a pool of watery tomato sauce.

I remember one dinner in particular: a *whole* steamed fish, served on a styrofoam plate with scales, fins and coagulated eye-balls staring blankly back at me, with a side of boiled cabbage.

What ten-year-old wants to eat this? Hello, chef! What are you thinking?

After dinner, we took turns in the shower, had some sort of nighttime activity that didn't include food, and went to our beds with *Taps* blaring on the loudspeaker.

I cried myself to sleep every night.

Time Never Stops

I really struggled at fat camp. I cried constantly and begged to go home. I pleaded with people to call my parents, certain that if they knew how upset I really was, they would come and get me.

I didn't make friends, and in all honesty, I pushed people away. I didn't want to be there and was desperate to get out and go home. My mind was in overdrive trying to figure out what to do.

When it became apparent that no rescue was imminent, I came up with a phrase that got me through, moment by moment: *Time never stops.* I must have said this to myself a million times over the next two months, just to get through the most unimaginably horrible experience that was now my life.

Time never stops.

This was my security blanket. It was a reminder that even though my reality was nearly unbearable for me, it was closer to being over with each passing moment.

Time never stops.

It was on repeat in my head. Every second passing is a second closer to being out. *Now* was excruciating. *Later* would eventually be here.

In retrospect, I wasn't present. A ten-year-old shouldn't have to be "present," but certainly shouldn't be in so much emotional pain that she makes up a mantra to mentally catapult herself past it.

Kitty Clopper and the Nature Walk

There were two "morbidly obese" girls in residence at fat camp: me and Kitty Clopper*. Kitty Clopper was blonde, had a southern drawl, and some sort of palatal defect which caused her words to sound extremely nasal. At age ten, Kitty weighed more than 200 pounds and was not very active.

In our entrance assessments, the camp nurse diagnosed both Kitty and I as "morbidly obese." Even in fat camp we were freaks! The other kids made fun of us, and we sometimes made fun of each other. But since we also had this rare distinction in common, we often stood together. We were frenemies.

One day, we all went for a nature walk down a wooded trail. I liked walking under the tall trees. Looking up at the sky, I noticed how the branches and leaves created the most beautiful patterns of mottled light on the ground. I watched the patterns of light move on my skin as I walked. "My grandma is under this same sky right now," I thought to myself. This always brought me comfort.

But today, I was walking with Kitty. As the two heaviest girls in the camp, we kept the same pace in the back of the line. Coming around a bend, I noticed the light reflecting off something purple in a pile of leaves at the base of a tree.

I looked more closely. I couldn't believe my eyes. Someone had dropped a giant-sized tube of *Bonne Bell Lip-Smacker*, in the most delicious of all flavors: Grape!

I glanced at Kitty Clopper and watched as the realization of what we'd stumbled upon registered in her eyes. She, too, was looking at the tube of Lip Smacker, wide-eyed, mouth hanging open, gaze transfixed. I knew that she wanted it as much as I did. We both urgently lumbered to the purple tube and dove on it together. Leaves blew up in the air and the tube rolled just out of reach. We wrestled one another, trying to hold each others' arms back, hoping we would each get to the coveted tube first. Victoriously, I grabbed the lip-smacker, snapped off the cap, and took a big bite. Even as I was chewing it, Kitty was trying to wrestle it out of my hands.

Names have been changed.

Weigh-In

Wednesdays were weigh-in days for our bunkhouse. We lined up at the nurse's office. She stood by a tall metal Holbert scale, with an assistant stationed at a nearby table with our weight history cards and a pencil.

As we approached our turn on the scale, we each stripped down to our underwear and stepped on the scale. The nurse yelled out our weight to her assistant to enter on the card. The assistant yelled back to the nurse whether the new weight was higher or lower than last week's.

Even though I was losing weight, I felt humiliated. My weight, something that I avoided knowing myself, was announced for everyone in the room to hear. And the whole "lining-up naked" thing reminded me of the horrible movies I saw in Sunday school about the Holocaust. Even though I tried my best to cover myself with my arms, the other girls stared at my naked, fat body with a combination of shock and curiosity.

Collect Call from Amy

We were allowed to call home once a week, on Sunday. Each bunk lined up at their assigned time, and every camper was allowed to talk for five minutes.

It was 1975, the era of the collect call. To make a collect call, I went to the outdoor camp pay phone, inserted my dime, and dialed zero to be connected to an operator. I told her I was making a collect call, and gave her my home phone number and my first name. When someone answered, the operator asked them if they would accept the charges for a collect call from Amy. Once they accepted, my line was connected and I could talk to them.

I called home a couple of consecutive Sundays. I begged my mom to let me come home, since I wasn't sleeping much, didn't have friends, and missed my grandma terribly.

She refused.

The next Sunday, when the operator asked my mom if she would accept a collect call from Amy, she said no and hung up . . . twice. So, I tried my grandma's telephone number. As soon as my grandma heard the operator start to speak, she cleverly made use of the few seconds that I could hear her while the operator attempted to verify charges, and frantically started speaking: "Amy, I love you so much and miss you! Your parents won't let me accept your calls!"

The phone went dead and I became a fat camp orphan.

From the end of June until the day before school started, when I went back home, no one from home was allowed to talk to me.

At ten years old, I felt marginalized, unwanted, and abandoned.

This devastating sense of isolation and punishment due to being fat created overwhelming angst and feelings of powerlessness around food and being overweight. It was all part of the painful emotional and physical punishment related to obesity that voraciously consumed me for decades to come.

Cape Cod

Up until that summer, my family spent summers on Cape Cod. My mom, sister, grandma and I went to the Cape each year. My dad would stay home, work during the week and visit on weekends. Sometimes, a friend from home would come with me and we would go outside all day to enjoy the beach. As a kid, I was a strong swimmer and spent hours in the water. It made me feel weightless. I could move about freely—floating, diving and swimming all day.

While I was at fat camp, one of my sisters was on Cape Cod. She got a summer job making donuts. Not just any donuts, Antonio's* donuts, the most popular donuts on the Cape. Light and well-cooked, never greasy. Frosted, sprinkled, sugared, stuffed with jelly, Boston Cream! Even Antonio's plain donuts were delicious.

My sister mailed me the occasional letter from Cape Cod. These letters usually included how she spent her days, "lying on the beach all day, listening to the radio, getting a tan, and lightening my hair with lemon juice," followed by the words, "If I never see another chocolate frosted donut with sprinkles again, it will be too soon!" In one letter, replete with grease stains and chocolate smudges, she drew herself as a stick figure with a donut for a body, along with a simple arrow, labeling it, "Me." If I sniffed hard enough, I could almost taste one of Antonio's donuts.

*Names have been changed.

The Peach

Food was prohibited in the fat camp bunkhouse. We couldn't be trusted with food, so snacks were totally off-limits. Once, I smuggled a peach out of the dining hall and put it on the window sill near my bed. I wanted to eat that peach in the morning, by myself, in peace, and on my terms.

I hated being hungry most of the time.

I knew it was going to be the perfect summer peach—the kind that when I bit into it, the juice would run down my arm. I went to sleep dreaming about that peach and how wonderful it smelled and how I would be in control over what I ate first thing in the morning. When I woke up, I reached up to get that peach. Something was wrong! It was all sticky! I looked closer. It had two little claw marks on each side of it with long bite marks up and down the peel.

A bat ate my peach.

After that, I slept with the sleeping bag zipped-up over my head.

Movie Night

One night a week, we watched a movie and were given a three-ounce cup of unsalted popcorn, about twenty kernels. I made this last for the entire movie, even if it was two hours long. The first week, we watched *Chitty Chitty Bang Bang*. I think they were trying to lull us into a false sense of security because the second week, the movie was *Cool Hand Luke*.

For a ten-year-old kid, a movie about men in prison was terrifying—yet somehow, I could totally relate.

Family Day

"Tan people look nice and slim!" the camp counselors exuberantly told us, as they directed us to lay in the sun after swimming so we would get tan. It was the week before Family Day, the midway point for the fat camp season. It was the one and only day during the summer when everyone's family was allowed to visit and see how much weight we had lost.

They brought gifts like stuffed animals and *Mad Libs*, and smaller clothes to wear, since the clothes we brought with us were falling off our shrinking bodies. The camp planned a special menu of barbecued hamburgers on white buns, macaroni salad with real mayonnaise, rippled potato chips, and soft serve ice cream. So, I got a tan, or rather a sunburn that *became* a tan, and I fantasized about my parents taking me home with them in a dramatic rescue.

But on Family Day, no one came to visit me.

A week later, I received a letter from my mom:

> *Dear Amy,*
> *We didn't come see you because it would have upset you too much. Stay there. Lose weight. We will pick you up at the end of camp right before school starts. Keep up the good work!*

By this time, other kids were telling their parents about me, my unusual homelife, how I cried a lot, and was homesick. Some of their moms noticed that no one came to see me on

Family Day. One girl's mother started to write to me on beautiful monogrammed stationery. She asked about my favorite things during Family Day and mailed me a package containing extra-large safety pins to hold up my shorts, a stuffed animal, a mood pen that changed colors as I wrote, three of my favorite peanut butter candy bars, and some spicy cinnamon candies.

Oddly enough, lots of parents sent their kids to fat camp, then smuggled junk food to them in care packages. Anyway, I had a pen pal! She wrote to me and I wrote back. She even sent me some of my own special stationery with an "A" on it and postage stamps so I could correspond with her. Every so often, I spoke to her on Sundays when her daughter called home.

I felt really special.

Another World

Speaking of letters, my grandma loved to watch daytime television and her favorite soap opera was *Another World*. When she wrote to me at fat camp, the letters would go something like this:

> *Dear Amy,*
> *Rachel and Mac broke-up and Sven is holding Rachel hostage in a shed in the woods. Mac doesn't know she's there and thinks she has left the country for good. He is brokenhearted as Rachel is the love of his life. Joey Perinni is putting poison in Ada's coffee every morning, telling her it's a saccharine tablet, and it's making her go blind. Joey is in love with Rachel and is conspiring with Sven to hold her hostage in the cabin…*

One Happy Memory

I do have one happy memory from fat camp. I excelled at archery. I achieved Sharp Shooter status for my age group. I loved archery! It was the one sport that didn't require me to run.

'Twas the Night before Freedom

On the final night of fat camp, we had a campwide dinner, complete with an awards ceremony, a talent show, and, to our surprise, a visit from the owner of fat camp! She arrived fashionably late in a flurry of excitement. She was slim and wore a light blue sequined dress, silver high-heeled sandals, a mile-high, pitch black, bouffant hairdo, bright pink frosted lipstick, and a megawatt smile. From the stage, she congratulated us for our collective weight loss and encouraged us to continue to diet and lay in the sun, because "tan people look nice and slim!" She assured us that when our parents picked us up the next morning, our new bodies would make them very proud.

After the ceremony, we each lined up and had a souvenir photo taken with her. I wore a dingy t-shirt and yellow polyester shorts held up by safety pins.

She was very tan.

Back Home

The day before school started in September, my parents picked me up from camp in The Daddy Caddy. They congratulated me on my weight loss. They said I looked tan and nice and slim! Looking at my official "before and after" fat camp photos, I, too, noticed the change. I lost twenty-six pounds in eight weeks, all at the age of ten. I got to ride in the front seat again, but this time we drove straight to a local fried fish restaurant. My mom ordered me a Fried Chicken Deluxe Platter: delicious golden fried chicken, thick cut french fries, and a mountain of onion rings, accompanied by a tall double-chocolate shake.

I gained fifty pounds during the next school year and was sent away to a different fat camp the following summer. This became my cycle: Lose weight under duress, with a plan that felt like punishment, filled with tricks and trauma, only to fail and gain back every pound I'd lost. This, ultimately, was unsustainable.

First Day of School

When I walked down the hall on the first day of school after that miserable summer at fat camp, my favorite teacher stood outside her classroom and clapped for the slimmer me. This probably should have made me feel great, but what I heard inside my head was, "I was not acceptable before. She likes me a lot better like *this*!"

Stripped

One week after fat camp, as the newest ten-year-old lifetime member of our local community weight loss program, I attended my first public meeting.

Institutionalized and dehumanized, I stripped down to my underwear in a room full of adult strangers to line up and get weighed. The meeting leader rushed over to me covering my body saying, "Oh, no, Amy! We don't do that here!"

After a few weeks of consistent weight gain, my parents stopped taking me to meetings.

School

My mom packed lunches for me like a toasted bagel with cream cheese and lox or a tuna fish sandwich. Boys frequently stole my lunch from my locker and threw the bag down the hall, taking turns stomping on it, so I couldn't eat. When this got reported to the principal, he called me into his office and told me, "I hear people are stealing your lunches. Well, you're known for eating good food. Maybe they are jealous."

The boys who took my lunches didn't stop with just taking my lunches. They made a game out of shoving each other or other students into me—as hard as they could—as they shouted, "Wide load!" This took place in the hallways between classes. Sometimes I saw it coming, and braced myself against the locker as fast as I could to minimize the blow. Other times, it took me by surprise and I would drop all my school books as I slammed into the lockers. This continued right up through high school and was just another humiliating thing I had to navigate in my everyday world because of my weight.

Gym

For a fat kid, gym class was torture. I felt embarrassed changing my clothes in front of the other girls in the locker room. They would blatantly stare at me, so I moved into the bathroom and disrobed in there. We didn't have school gym uniforms, so my mom had to find shorts that would fit me. This was the 1970s and plus size clothing stores didn't exist the way they do today. My mom found me a pair of men's size 2x white shorts with dark blue piping. She could only find one pair, so I had to wear them a couple of days in a row, then bring them home for her to wash. After a few weeks, they shrunk—or maybe I gained weight—and they got a yellow tinge from the bleach she used trying to keep them white. It didn't matter. Once I figured out how to forge my mom's signature, I just wrote excuses to get out of gym class and sit on the bleachers until gym class was over.

Trick-Or-Treat

Living in a small town, we went trick-or-treating on Hallow-een. Our family doctor lived right up the street. I was out with some other kids and we knocked on his door. I felt proud that I knew who lived there and that we were visiting the home of our family doctor. I couldn't wait to show him my costume! When he opened the door, holding a bowl of full-size candy bars, he scolded me. "You don't need candy, Amy. I'm calling your parents. Go home."

OVERWEIGHT: A MEMOIR OF DIS-EASE

I Didn't Fit

There were a bunch of things I didn't fit into and had to plan for ahead of time. This made me anxious about being in those situations. I didn't fit into chairs with attached desks. I had to bend my knees and stuff myself sideways into them. My hips would touch the bus seats when I walked down the center aisle of the school bus. I opted to sit up front near the bus driver to avoid that shameful walk, and to be somewhat protected from the mean kids on the bus. One girl walked down the aisle, bouncing off of every seat before flopping into one, just to make fun of me. Yelling over uproarious laughter from the other kids on the bus, she hollered to me, "Why don't you just stop eating, Fatso!"

Kickball

One day after school, some neighborhood boys and girls were playing kickball in the parking lot behind the post office. To my surprise, one of the girls asked me if I wanted to join. They were one person short and trying to get a game going. She knew my name was Amy, but as I walked up to the plate to kick, she yelled to me: "Do you mind if I just call you Fatso? It's a lot easier to remember."

"Okay!" I agreed. I was just happy to have been included. The ball was rolled to me. Carrying around an extra hundred pounds made my legs really strong. I kicked as hard as I could, and that ball went flying! As I started to take off from homebase I heard her scream, "Run, Fatso! Jesus! You're not even going to make it to first base!"

I got quite accustomed to people sizing me up as "Fatso" instead of Amy. My weight problem was the whole of me. The inner me was silent.

Fat Joke

Somewhere around twelve years old, my parents took me to a female weight loss doctor. I changed into an exam gown that wasn't big enough to cover my body. I feared what she would recommend as the next round of torture in a futile attempt to lose weight. Having been in similar situations before, I decided to try to ingratiate myself to her, so that she might take mercy on me and my future. I made small talk and said something funny. She didn't laugh.

Instead, she sat on her rolling stool, moved toward me, crossed her arms and legs, leaned uncomfortably close to me, and inquired sternly in a thick German accent, "You seem unusually happy for someone as overweight as you. Are you trying to hide your deep feelings of shame with humor?"

For years after that, whenever I made a joke I wondered if I was just trying to make people like me because I was so fat.

What a Shame

I didn't realize it at the time, but the worst things that were ever said to me were permanently recorded in my brain for constant replay on my own abusive, internal soundtrack:

"You're fat and ugly."

"Nobody wants you around."

"You're a joke."

"You can't do anything right."

"You're a fat pig."

"Fatso!"

And I heard a many-a-veiled "compliment"—"What a shame. You have such a pretty face."

I must have heard this one a thousand times. I did have a pretty face . . . big, blue eyes and dark hair with pretty features and clear skin. Unfortunately, as I was so often reminded, it was all attached to my fat body.

I never stood up for myself. I never hit anyone who made fun of me, even though I towered over everyone until high school and was quite strong. No one ever stepped in to defend me. I just took the abuse . . . over and over. Their hatred of me beat me down. And I joined them in hating me.

I may have been physically large, but inside, I was small and helpless. And the constant external and internal abuse only made this worse.

The larger I got on the outside, the smaller I felt on the inside.

An Emerging Pattern

My experiences at fat camp, my daily struggles as a fat kid, and the dysfunction in my homelife solidified devastating eating issues for me.

I had a love-hate relationship with food.

My life sent me frantically looking for ways to deal with what I *couldn't* control—with the one thing I *could* control: what I put in my mouth. It worked right up until the next emotion.

On one hand, food was an instant relief, however fleeting, for any uncomfortable emotion. If I felt disappointed, scared or upset, helpless or hopeless, I turned to food. It was always there for me when I needed it.

But on the other hand, I needed food around me all the time, since I hated feeling even the least bit hungry, because hunger signaled punishment and deprivation. When I did eat, I immediately felt guilty and had to eat more to numb that uncomfortable emotion.

I lived in a grossly overweight body and had a total lack of nutritional understanding. I firmly believed that exercise was punishment, and I felt completely ashamed of how I looked. I dissociated from my physical body in order to survive, otherwise I never would have left my house.

I ate without thinking.

As I attempted to cope by ravenously consuming food, it, in turn, consumed me.

My Mom

My mom's middle name was McElwane*. When I asked her where this name came from, she explained that when her mother was pregnant with her, their childless neighbors, The McElwanes, asked my grandma to name my mom, McElwane. They allegedly promised to pay my grandma $250 so that their name would be carried on, even as a middle name for my mom. My grandma kept her side of the bargain. The McElwanes never paid. My mom was kind of screwed from birth.

She had a rough childhood. When she was a baby, her nineteen-year-old mother (my beloved grandma) permanently dropped her off at her parents' house. My mom never knew her father; he was kept away from her. Instead, her grandparents raised her while her mother lived a new life elsewhere.

Despite stories of being dirt poor, experiencing abuse including being locked in a dark closet for hours, terrified by someone dragging chains around and making scary noises to punish her, and being beaten with her grandmother's orthopedic shoe, she recounted those memories as part of a childhood for which she was grateful.

My mom was an only child and she thought back on that with tremendous loss and sadness. She missed out on having siblings—in her mind, who probably could have protected her. She used to say that she wanted a dozen kids and settled for a half-dozen. I think she thought that having kids would fill the void.

It didn't.

My mom was slim and had an hourglass figure. She was gorgeous: Greek with olive skin, dark eyes and a bright smile. When she wore a gown, she looked like she just stepped out of a Hollywood movie. And the only makeup she ever wore was her signature hot pink lipstick. She cared about her figure and her appearance. She was known as one of the most beautiful women around. Imagine her distaste when she brought me clothes shopping in the "pleasantly plump" section. That's what it was called—pleasantly plump. But there was nothing 'pleasant' about it, for her, or for me.

Out of nowhere, like a surprise inspection, my mom would direct me to "T-T-I!" This was her secret code for "tuck tummy in," which meant she wanted me to suck my stomach in, because I looked fat. "T-T-I!" could happen anytime and anywhere—while posing for a family photo, at the grocery store, even playing with friends. It was a secret code between us and reminded me that I was not acceptable as I was.

My mom had many wonderful gifts.

She was truly masterful with words and could create delightfully clever rhymes, poems and songs on the spot. She had the most gorgeous handwriting—beautifully executed strings of letters with pointed tips and perfectly formed bodies. She had a sharp wit and a sharper tongue. She loved babies.

She lived like she had something to prove. She once bought a set of enormous, heavy andirons for the fireplace. Instead of asking my dad for help carrying them into the house, she did it herself. I could barely budge them and she carried them all the way into the living room from the car. It took her two hours. All because she wouldn't ask for help.

She once wrestled a male gorilla and saved a child's life.

My mom was creative. She sewed gingham fabric envelopes with beautifully written invitations for my grade school birthday party. She made sure every child in my class was included. For a history project in grade school, she baked a three-foot-tall cake that was a scale replica of the Parthenon that she had me pass off as my homework assignment when we were studying Greek columns in history. And she was a great cook. For special family dinners, she made food from all over the world: Spanish Paella, fork-tender pot roast, Chinese food (eaten only with chopsticks for culture), flaming Baked Alaska, Portuguese soup, a huge meal she called the Greek Feast, and the best apple pie in the world. My mom's ability to cook delicious international foods in her rural kitchen would define me as a foodie for life.

Names have been changed.

The Family Secret

My mom's alcoholism was a family secret. I had to pretend to the outside world that everything at home was fine. I wasn't allowed to talk about her drinking with other people. We rarely even acknowledged it in our own family. My mom's emotional and sometimes physical state was fragile and violent. My very world revolved around whether or not she was drunk.

I have lots of memories of my mom and her issues around drinking. She kept a fifth of vodka in the chamber of each of her grandfather clocks (she had three) and took five gulps every time she passed by. "I'm a counter," she told me during one of her rehab stints. She always counted the five gulps going down.

My mom sometimes worked with my dad at his office. This arrangement was on and off. As I got older, she worked more. But as a kid, each day when I got off the bus, I'd see my mom outside the house waiting for me. I could tell from one hundred yards away if she was drunk or sober because she had a facial tick when she was drunk. I knew from that tick what sort of night it was going to be.

One day I got off the bus from grade school, and she wasn't there waiting for me. I thought it was odd, but walked up the long driveway home. The door was unlocked. I heard water running in the downstairs bathroom. I called for my mom and heard a very faint, "I'm in here."

I could tell by her voice she'd been drinking.

I opened the bathroom door to find her sitting naked in a tub full of bloody water. She held up her arms wrapped with blood-soaked gauze bandages. She had slit her wrists and bandaged them up. She was, after all, a licensed practical nurse.

"Oh, don't worry," she slurred, her eyes drunkenly trying to find mine, "If I really wanted to kill myself I would have." This was the first of two bloody failed suicide attempts I discovered as a child, both by her slitting her wrists in the bathtub.

When she drank heavily for days on end, she hallucinated. One of the scariest things I remember was the time she thought she was speaking with Russian agents through her bedside alarm clock and believed she was ordered to carry out a hit on my dad. She hid a new axe under their bed, retrieved it, and chased him through the house swinging it wildly at him, swearing she would kill him. After a good ten minutes of screaming, chasing, and swinging, during which I hid crouched in the corner of my clothes closet, he ran out the front door and drove to a local motel where he stayed for several days.

On his way out of the house he yelled to me to "watch her." I was eleven years old.

Years later in therapy, after I'd had my own son, I shared this memory with my therapist and sort of brushed it off. My therapist asked me if I would ever leave my eleven-year-old son home with his other parent swinging an axe at me. Only when she asked me this, did I fully understand the craziness that I grew up in. At the time, I thought it was completely normal.

My dad stayed away when my mom drank heavily, leaving me at home with her. I was forced to be the adult. As a child, I took care of her. I determined the safety in the home, I made sure she didn't hurt herself, I made sure she didn't try to drive, and I kept it all a secret.

The stress was overwhelming. I turned to food to make it through. If I felt upset, I would eat. Nervous? *Eat.* Annoyed? *Eat.* Disappointed? *Eat.* Scared? *Eat.* Overwhelmed? *Eat.*

Food was the only coping mechanism I knew. It neutralized the present uncomfortable feeling and worked right up until the next. Unfortunately, the feelings were coming at me through a firehose.

You Drive Me to Drink

My mom was drunk, but decided she needed to go somewhere. My best friend and I were playing in the house when she told us to get in the car. My mom drove a wood-paneled station wagon with a bench-style front seat. My mom got behind the wheel, my friend was sitting in the middle seat, and I was in the passenger seat.

We were driving down a busy two-lane highway. There was a pedestrian walking toward us on the right-hand shoulder. As we got closer, my mom wasn't moving away from the shoulder to give the pedestrian room. A few feet from hitting the pedestrian, my friend grabbed the steering wheel out of instinct and moved the car to the left, just missing the pedestrian.

My mom pulled over and yelled at my friend for grabbing the wheel screaming, "Don't ever do that! How dare you! Never touch the steering wheel!" My friend saved that person's life.

Another time, my mom drove drunk to our local gas station and hit the gas pump, knocking it off the concrete pad. She didn't know what she'd done and drove home. Moments later, the police arrived at our house to investigate. Because of who my dad was in the community, they didn't arrest her or charge her with anything. That's the night I decided I needed to do the driving. I was eleven.

She once told me, "You drive me to drink! The doctors were right. After my car accident, they told me not to have any more children. Then I got pregnant with you. The doctors told me to abort you and I fought to keep you. But look at you." Her eyes slowly perused my overweight body, in an exaggeratedly slow fashion, toe to head. "I've created a monster!"

I learned years later that the year before I was born, she broke both hips driving drunk.

It's All in My Head

My mom always denied being drunk. She hid her alcohol and drank secretly. Her drink of choice was vodka, because she claimed it had no odor and couldn't be detected. She didn't seem to realize that her drunken actions gave her away. When she was drinking, she had that facial tick, a weird fake laugh, and smoked cigarettes.

The most damaging thing for me was her outright denial that she was drinking at all. If I asked her about it (which was a terrifying act in itself, since she held grudges and reacted violently to being accused of drinking), she called me crazy, told me I was imagining things, and that it was all in my head. Never, in all the time she was drinking, did she admit it to me. As a child, I was completely confused. Was I crazy? Did I know how to discern information accurately? Was I unsafe with her as I thought, or was I making things up and blowing everything out of proportion?

These experiences with my mom left me emotionally disabled in terms of my ability to authentically interact with other people. For decades, I doubted what I saw, thought and felt. Or worse, blamed myself for anything wrong around me.

I'm pretty sure my mom's alcoholism had something to do with my weight problem. My best guess is, I didn't get unconditional love from her, so I didn't think I had the ability to be loved, even and especially by myself.

Food became a reliable way to distract, medicate, distance, and prove my perceived worthlessness to myself and anyone around me.

The only thing that relieved all this angst was a visit with my grandma, my mom's mother—Mary, whom we nicknamed Happy. My goal, after making sure my mom was safe, was to get upstairs where my grandma lived, as quickly as I could and stay there until I got called downstairs for dinner. That's when my dad came home. That's when I wouldn't be alone with my mom.

My Grandma, "Happy"

My grandma lived with us in a few private rooms upstairs. She wore a housecoat and a big diamond ring on her pinky. She had white hair and beautiful green eyes. She wore silver "cat-eye glasses." She was petite and plump. She had been married three times. She spent her days doing crossword puzzles at a metal kitchen table in her apartment.

She had a small galley kitchen with butter out on the counter all the time, because room temperature butter was supremely spreadable, preferably a quarter-inch thick and served on a thin, salty cracker. When I visited her each day after school, she made me a butter-laden, grilled cheese sandwich with white bread and American cheese, and she had an endless supply of my favorite candy bars in her kitchen drawer. She bought me new magic markers and jumbo pads of coloring paper. She snoozed in a brown reclining chair while I colored and watched my favorite after-school television shows.

She was my safety, my haven, my best friend, and in hindsight, the only person who ever loved me unconditionally in my life. She was my heart and I was hers.

She let me play with her costume jewelry. She had a beautiful black lacquer jewelry box with a geisha inside which turned on a pedestal to the song *Sayonara* when I opened the lid. She had matching clip-on earrings and necklaces in every color, from black to aurora borealis; from plain to sparkly.

We also played school. She let me be the teacher and I corrected her crossword puzzles. For every space that wasn't filled, she lost one point. She almost always got 100%. Another favorite game was "ice cream store," where we would pretend that I ran an ice cream shop and she would order a special humdinger sundae, all made with mud, sticks, and maple tree helicopters.

My grandma wore full upper and lower dentures. To make me laugh, she would flip them in and out of her mouth. This was often done while lying back in her brown cloth recliner. The thought of it still makes me laugh today! She had her hair done at the hairdressers once a week. It was fine and white and done in a permanent. She showered with a plastic showercap so "it wouldn't get mussed."

To me, she was just beautiful.

I remember the smell of her skin. It was a mixture of Lily of the Valley and Kent cigarettes. I used to paint her fingernails. She used a white cuticle pencil and ran it under the ends of her nails to make the underside look white since they were stained yellow from nicotine. She used to smoke on the porch in her housecoat and diamond ring. She wasn't allowed to smoke inside the house. Ironically, my mom forbade it because she thought it was unhealthy for me.

I slept across the hall from my grandma's bedroom where I could hear her snoring. It didn't bother me at all. In fact, it was comforting for me to hear her. It let me know that I was safe.

She was really good to me. I wonder if it was her way of trying to mend her broken relationship with my mom. Either way, I loved her a lot.

Being somewhat plump, my grandma was a serial dieter. Food was either "legal" or "illegal," as she put it. All dressed up, polyester pantsuit, necklace, matching clip-on earrings, hair just so—she carpooled with friends to weekly community weight loss meetings. On their way home, they stopped for banana splits. For my grandma, dieting was more social than anything else.

Through all the decades she lived in our house, she was never invited to have dinner with us downstairs.

My Grandma's Death

My grandma was my security blanket in a crazy home life. More than that, she was effectively my stable parent. She died when I was sixteen years old. And she died alone.

My grandma was in the hospital for a few weeks. I'm not sure if anyone knew how near death she was. Someone said she had cancer. I was never given any details about her health, despite being the person with whom she was closest. I had seen her once in the hospital when she was admitted. I was home with my dad and mom—who at this point, was drunk more often than she was sober.

We got a call from the hospital that my grandma wasn't doing well. I remember the nurse saying, "she's cribbing back and forth in bed like a caged animal." We were gathering our things to go to the hospital when the phone rang. Our family doctor said she was gone.

My world shattered. My mom took her glasses off, stood in front of her mirrored-vanity and started sobbing. I ran outside without a coat into the frigid January night air and straight to my best friend's house. Her mom answered the door. I told her that my grandma died. She sat me down at their metal kitchenette table with a glass of cherry soda. She sat right next to me and comforted me while I cried. I cried that my grandma was so sick and all alone. I cried that I wasn't able to see her or be with her. I cried that I would be left to fend for myself at home. I cried because I was afraid of how my life would change without her. And I knew that my world became a lot less loving that night.

As devastated as I was, I kept the family secret.

I walked home to find a fire roaring in the fireplace and my very drunk mom. I said something to her about how drunk she was. I asked why we didn't get to see grandma in the hospital. She hit me so hard across the face that I fell to the ground. She walked away. If I expected her to comfort me, I was wrong.

My parents went to my grandma's funeral and burial alone. It wasn't a normal family funeral; my sisters and brothers didn't go, no celebration of life was held. And it was five hours away in New Jersey. I was left out, once again, because "it would upset me." Our cleaning lady stayed with me and she made spaghetti and meatballs with garlic bread. She hugged me a lot and we cried together. She was also very fat and loved my grandma a lot.

I continue to cling to the love my grandma shared with me throughout my life. I know what it feels like to have been truly loved by someone, no matter what.

My Dad

My dad was a great guy. I consider him my hero. He was a creative person and problem-solver. He was an eternal optimist. He loved to read. He was very intelligent. But he was also a lot of fun and effortlessly became the center of any gathering. He lit up the room.

By profession, he was a dentist who loved his craft. He took excellent care of people in the community, and was well-known for his philanthropy. He served in the United States Army in World War II in support of General Patton.

Being Jewish, he experienced anti-Semitism firsthand, and made it a point to raise us to treat everyone equally. He taught me, "There are good and bad people from all backgrounds and walks of life. You can never judge a group of people based on the actions of one." He also taught me how to treat people in general. "No matter what, you can always find something nice to say to them. It makes them feel good."

When he wasn't wearing his dental smock, he wore bib overalls and an old, white t-shirt. He never showed up *anywhere* empty-handed. A bushel of just-picked apples, a loaf of rye bread, a couple of lobsters from the Cape—wherever he went, he brought a gift to whomever he was visiting, and it was almost always food.

My dad loved to eat. He had a *pupek* as he called it—a belly. He had strong legs and a big tummy, the pupek. Looking back, I think he, too, ate out of habit and stress. He certainly loved good food, but he also ate secretly and under duress.

Despite being a brilliant man, my dad never figured out how to effectively deal with my mom's alcoholism. At that time, being an alcoholic carried a terrible social stigma and my dad had an important role in the community. He knew that fighting with my mom about her drinking led nowhere, and all he ever really wanted was peace. Consequently, she ran roughshod over him.

I remember them having the occasional shouting match, so it's not like they didn't fight, but as out-of-control as she was, he never threw down the gauntlet and said, "Stop it or else!" I think sometimes, he was rightfully afraid of her. But at all times, he remained deeply compassionate with her, being acutely aware of her upbringing and her painful history. He knew her better than anyone. He understood that at the core of her raging alcoholism, she was a wounded child—fragile and delicate. Any serious repercussions to her behavior would devastate her completely.

He loved her.

So, he danced with her . . . her alcoholism, how she treated their children, and how her addiction affected everyone in their lives.

In our family, good food was important. My dad installed a grill in the outside smokehouse where he fried hotdogs. He slathered the buns with butter and grilled them, too! We had extra freezers out there filled with food, and, like many families in that era, shelves of food in the basement in case of a nuclear war.

My dad used to get up in the middle of the night to eat. Sometimes, he'd make a pot of oatmeal that was waiting on the stove the next morning. He also made amazing roast beef, covered with a salt and pepper crust. He made the best ever horseradish, "Doc's Dynamite," that we probably could have packaged and sold.

Sunday dinners in my teens were really great. We would all meet and eat—including my siblings who lived nearby. As the youngest child of six by many years (my siblings ranged from seven to nineteen years older than me), I never lived under the same roof with most of them. I knew them only as adults. Those Sunday dinners gave me a sense of what it must have been like to have siblings at home and not just be a "late in life, only child," left to fend for herself. Food was the center of those events and I look back happily on them. Having a food-centric family would later serve me well in figuring out successful ways to make healthy versions of food profiles that I loved.

My dad taught me a lot of great things.

His practice of finding something nice to say about everyone helped me to find the best in people throughout my life. He was a true optimist who always found the good in a situation. He loved to laugh and his laughter was contagious. He had a huge *Qi* or life force; so charismatic and caring that many called him the father of the village. People were drawn to him. It was natural. He never tried. He never boasted. He never said, "Hey, look at what I did!" He saw the potential in people and helped them quietly, and when they did succeed, he never took any credit.

My dad sometimes socialized me like a boy. He taught me how to drive a tractor as a child, and brought me into the garden with him to help dig up potatoes in the fall. I knew how to drive a car at eleven years old, and when I got my learner's permit, he took me out on a four-lane highway and taught me about "city driving." He had a keen interest in politics and current events and often explained what was happening in the world during the nightly news broadcast. Most importantly, though, he advised me to be self-sufficient and never to rely on other people for anything I wanted or needed.

My dad believed that education was sacred, saying, "Learn as much as you can." Recounting to me what happened to Jews during World War II he added, "Education can never be taken away from you." My dad grew in his thoughts throughout his life. He never stagnated in his thinking and loved to talk with other intelligent people about current events or travel. He was a voracious reader, and when I say voracious, I mean he read one novel each day up until he passed.

My dad taught me about business, too. He taught me to invest in myself and my own business, and to be my own boss. Experiencing anti-Semitism first hand, he advised me to work for myself so that others couldn't hold me back due to their own prejudices. He also taught me to "pay myself first" as a way to save money. He helped me invest in real estate, which he called the best investment of all. And, "never buy something on a credit card that you can't pay for outright," he warned. "That's a trap that ultimately makes a fifty-dollar pair of shoes cost you five-hundred dollars!" He taught me how to create and manage my own economy and advised me not to loan friends money; "That always turns out bad," he cautioned.

He was curious about life and had a bright outlook. One day, I found him searching the internet for "how to live to be one hundred." He was ninety one years old.

He enjoyed peace and the simple things in life. He loved a good cup of coffee. He would sip from his mug and sigh, "Ahhhhh, *mechaya*," Yiddish for "What a true pleasure!"

He told a good joke.

He was Jewish, but had a decidedly eastern philosophy about life.

When I was twenty two years old, I was invited to a wake. This was my first time seeing a dead body. I was scared and didn't know what to expect, so I talked to my dad. I figured that he had seen a dead body or two and hoped that he could help brace me for seeing my first deceased person.

He took this opportunity to first share his belief that the human body is miraculous. He revealed his reverence and wonder that developed when he had to dissect cadavers in dental school as part of his training. Soon after, he joined the United States Army and served in World War II under General George Patton. He was the captain of a dental unit and part of the medical corps that administered medical and dental care to thousands of wounded soldiers in field hospitals. He learned an abundance of real-world techniques for restorative and prosthetic dentistry there. He was proud to later use those experiences to creatively and skillfully help people in our community with their dental needs.

He once happened upon a devastating car accident in which my brother's best friend was decapitated when a deer crashed through his windshield. He also served as the forensic dentist for an investigation and trial for a man who murdered his wife and small children, then threw their bodies into a well. His job was to positively identify the remains using their decomposed jaws and dental records.

He was no stranger to trauma and death.

So, as he prepared me for that first wake, he said, "I've seen a lot of dead bodies in my lifetime, and when my own mother died, I wanted to see her to say goodbye before they closed her in the coffin. She didn't want me to see her, but I really felt I needed to see her one last time. I wish I didn't. It was my mother, I know, but now every time I think of her, I remember her lying in her casket, lifeless."

He continued, "The soul rejoins the source at death. The body, when no longer animated by the spirit, is just a lump of clay. Do me a favor. Don't come see my dead body and don't cry at my gravestone when I'm gone. I'll be with you. Talk out loud to me and quiet your mind and listen. I will answer you."

My dad taught me how to live and later taught me how to die.

So much healing was yet to take place.

Teen Crushed

Life was moving on. I wasn't exactly the helpless girl I'd been in early childhood, but I wasn't thriving, either. I did have a couple of close girlfriends and we've remained dear friends into our adulthood. But I didn't date. If I developed a crush on someone, that affection was never returned. If someone found out about my crush on a boy, they teased him with the horrible news that he attracted me.

I was a curse.

Grave Mistake

There were many arguments with my mom as I entered my teens. I was bolder. I told her I knew she was drinking and I didn't back down. I don't know if this was to convince myself or her, but I held my ground and confronted her with her drunkenness many times.

I was a good student in school, but I struggled in my teens, especially with science. I did very poorly on a test once, and my science teacher called my parents, telling them that he suspected I was using drugs since I was "tired and out of it" during class. When I got home that day, my dad beat me with the belt. The beating was so bad that my mom excused me from gym for a couple of weeks so that no one would see the bruises and welts on my body. I got the belt several times in my life, but this was the worst, and I was beaten for something that didn't even happen. I wasn't the person using drugs, my mom was.

My mistake was in not doing a good job at keeping that a secret.

Years later, my dad apologized for beating me. We were sitting at the kitchen table at his house and I had a young son. He knew we didn't hit him and began reflecting. "Please don't think back on me as an abusive father," he said. "I did to you what was done to me, and I now know that it was wrong. I would hate for you to remember me that way."

Finally, after decades of physical and emotional abuse that was never mentioned, I gratefully accepted his apology. It was the best he could do. And it was the only admission or acknowledgement I ever got.

Unable to Break the Cycle

I stopped weighing myself at 311 pounds. I was nineteen years old. I'm sure my highest weight was much greater than 311 pounds. I didn't check.

The only clothing that fit me was a size 4x shirt that was designed to be a beach coverup for a regular-sized person. It fit me like a t-shirt. I wore men's size 48 pants.

Food was my constant companion. It was all I had. I was morbidly obese and had given up.

And as an adult, nobody could send me away anywhere or force me to do any dieting, ever again. I still lived at home, as dysfunctional as that was. I commuted to community college, since I didn't have the self-esteem to leave and attend college as all my siblings had done. Going away to college somehow felt scary, like fat camp. So, I worked on earning my degree during the day, and held down several part time jobs, proud of being able to help people. I was a really good worker—conscientious, eager to please, smart, helpful, and reliable.

Inside my head, though, it was an entirely different story. My negative self-talk was now a full-blown, twenty-four-hour, seven-days-a-week internal abuser. I was saying things to myself that I would never even *think* of saying to someone else. And my thoughts grew much darker:

"You're a loser, a failure, a joke."

"You are unlovable."

"No one will ever love you."

"Your mom is right, you are a monster."

"You were never meant to be here."

"You should be dead."

Distortion

Any time people took pictures, I tried my best to disappear. I couldn't bear to see myself in photos and felt dissociated from my body. I had no mirrors in my room, other than one in which I could see "my pretty face." It was devastating to visit a dressing room with a three-way mirror. I once broke down in a department store when I saw what I looked like partially naked from behind. It was harrowing to me—I was huge and wide with a roll of fat around my hips where my shirt got hung up. My thighs were large and dimpled and misshapen, and although I had a waistline, it was beneath three rolls of fat on my back.

My shoes stretched out to accommodate my feet. From carrying extra weight, my feet rolled outward. From this misalignment, my shoes took on an oval shape as I wore them. I remember feeling bad looking at my misshapen shoes waiting for me on the shoe mat every day.

Distorted shoes. Distorted body. Distorted mind. I was deformed.

A freak.

An accident.

A monster.

I Still Didn't Fit

As a 300-plus-pound adult, there were many things I didn't fit into: airplane seats, airplane seat belts, turnstyles, college chairs with attached desks, plastic patio chairs at friends' houses, theater seats. To my horror, I once broke a new friend's plastic toilet seat. If I went to a beach, I remained fully clothed. Otherwise, people stared. I know how it feels when every face on the beach, even people just passing by, are turned my way to look at me. A three hundred-plus-pound person on the beach can be a spectacle.

Social Misfit

I wouldn't go on a date until I was twenty four years old. I felt very lonely. If I liked someone, it was a source of embarrassment for them. Their friends would tease them that they attracted me. So other than school or work, I didn't venture out much, except with people I trusted to allow me to leave if I wasn't comfortable or didn't feel safe.

I remember once being at an out of town, New England-style restaurant with friends—an older couple. We decided to eat at a table in the restaurant's tavern. We were seated twenty feet from the bar, and there were two guys there, drinking beer and carrying on. When they saw me squeeze into the wooden captain's chair, their wisecracks began. Their remarks were somewhat quiet at first, but I was acutely aware of them as they hardily joked about me breaking the chair, and asking the bartender if they had enough food in the restaurant to feed me.

Their abusive commentary of me grew louder and more raucous until other diners noticed it, too. When one of them pointed at me and shouted to a friend across the bar, "If you want to fuck that fat pig, you're going to have to roll her in flour and look for the wet spot!", I burst into tears and ran from the restaurant. I was, to my core, fearful and ashamed. I knew that my obesity brought me disgust, disdain and verbal abuse. But this threat of violence from strangers escalated my feelings of grotesqueness to a new high, convincing me that I didn't fit in society.

Men weren't the only adults to point out my weight problem. Once at a steakhouse, an attractive blonde woman on a bar stool surrounded by men, used her wiles to point me out to her hangers-on, asking them if they'd ever seen anything so disgusting. She used their collective disgust in me, the fat girl, to ingratiate and underline her beauty and attractiveness to them. And it worked like a charm. They all pointed and laughed at me. This identical situation would happen again, in another restaurant, in another town, at another time, with other people.

Unsolicited Advice

Strangers gave me unsolicited nutritional advice. One man, staring at me putting salad on my plate in a buffet said, "You want to lose weight? Look down at your plate and put half of that back."

In college, a new, popular girlfriend tried to help me improve my social life. She said, "Lose a hundred pounds and someone might want to date you. Nobody I know would now."

She was right.

One Hell of a Show

During one of his late-in-life performances at a local fairground, a well-known, fifties era pop star rallied the outdoor, standing-room-only crowd to find fat people among them and send them up on stage to make them dance to his biggest hit for everyone's entertainment. People started yelling at me, "Hey, he wants all you fat people up on stage!" as they pushed and herded me in that direction. My sister was with me and, like me, was terrified. We managed to break out of the frenzied crowd and run to our car.

This hellish scene, straight out of my worst nightmare, was outlandish, unfathomable and harmful. It was then that I realized that my looks could endanger those around me whom I loved.

Today, we are growing more aware of the harm that body shaming causes, but at that time, there was no consciousness around the horrible habit of *fat* shaming. It was totally acceptable to make fun of fat people. It was the one thing almost everyone could agree was funny.

Feeling like I was the object of disgust, disdain, and disrespect, my inner self shrunk more and more.

Punishment

Once in a while, my self-loathing led me to try a fad diet. For several days—or even weeks, I could keep my head in it, but the feeling that it wasn't going to work coupled with being hungry all the time, and feeling like I was again being punished around food inevitably derailed me.

Exercise to me was also punishment and something I considered a chore at best and torture at worst. I didn't know how to move in my extra large body and absolutely dreaded it. I had to be careful. With all the extra weight I'd been carrying, I started to experience back pain and weakness. A lack of mobility loomed large in my future.

I'd occasionally watch a television infomercial showcasing some-one's major weight loss success story, and be fiercely tempted to order their miracle product. I had such a longing to *be that person*, the woman who lost eighty-five pounds and now looked beautiful and happy in her wedding dress. It was a longing…a longing for a chance to make things right and finally lose weight.

Every New Year's Eve, I cried myself to sleep and promised myself that this would be the year I would finally lose weight. I'd swear that by this time next year, I will have lost weight. I'd be slim. I'd be healthy. I'd be *living*. I felt ashamed and disgusted that I didn't do what I'd promised myself twelve months ago. One New Year's Eve, I jumped out of bed and frantically did some jumping jacks and sit-ups, sobbing, tears rolling down my face, to prove that this was finally the year I was going to lose weight.

It never stuck.

From time to time, I started a new diet program. Whether it was a meal replacement shake, fasting, or pre-packaged meals, I followed it for a few days or even a couple of weeks. But inevitably, I lost motivation and felt like I was punishing myself. My inner voice brutally informed me that I couldn't do it, I didn't matter, I was destined to be fat, I was a failure, and I should just stop trying. The sense of deprivation, frustration, and lack of motivation always led me to give up and return to my regular, poor eating habits. In this cycle, I gained back everything I'd lost and more.

This pattern continued into my thirties, when I was able to lose forty pounds and get down to about two hundred seventy-five pounds. I met a wonderful man, got married, had a beautiful son, and stayed at that weight for years. I was "the fat mom" in my son's class and I hated that. I didn't want my limitations to spill over into my son's life, creating problems for him.

I knew my weight kept me from living my life the way I desperately wanted to.

With every fiber of my being, I wanted to do better. I wanted to be better.

Your turn to reflect.

"The larger I got on the outside, the smaller I felt on the inside."

How is your weight keeping *you* from living the life you want?

_____

_____

_____

_____

_____

_____

_____

_____

_____

_____

_____

_____

_____

_____

_____

CHAPTER 2

Finding My "Why": A Turning Point Toward Ease

My body totally hid and distorted who I was, the essential "me," the soul "me." If we are souls in meat suits, mine was so far out of whack on the outside from who I was on the inside, that it made daily life unbearable.

By this point in my life, I had tried and failed at dozens of diets. Shakes, boxed meals, fasting, counting points, the grapefruit diet, the banana diet, the cabbage soup diet—I tried them all and failed at them all.

But I also had something new. I was older and a bit wiser. I'd seen both of my parents live to a nice old age. If I, too, had a long life ahead of me, I contemplated how I wanted to grow old. I shuddered at the thought of being a 400-pound woman in a double-size wheelchair, being cared for in a nursing home, and having to be transported to the toilet in a Hoyer lift. I could see my own future clearly, and it wasn't one I wanted. I also had a son and wanted to do better, to be better for him and for me. I no longer found it acceptable to be "the fat mom." I was sick of hearing, "What a shame, you have such a pretty face." And most importantly, I was fed up with being stuck in a body that no longer aligned with how I envisioned my future.

In every other way, I was an accomplished woman. I had a kind husband and a beautiful son. I had successful businesses, I knew how to get things done at a high level of quality, and I succeeded at most things I tried.

But weight loss? It owned me.

Then it happened.

My dad was ninety-one when he fell and broke his hip.

He died one week later.

In the week leading up to his death, my dad underwent hip and leg repair surgery and was recovering in the hospital. Being a clinician all his life, I think he realized that he wasn't going to heal the way he wanted to, and knew he wouldn't return to an independent, mobile life.

We didn't know it at the time, but he planned to make his last moments with his children something special, something that would last a lifetime, our lifetimes. He spent one-on-one time with each of us, talking about what he thought our biggest challenge was in life, and through seemingly spontaneous conversations with each of us, he gently offered advice on how we might overcome it.

He asked me to bring my thirteen-year-old son to him in the hospital. "Can you bring Levi here for a visit?" he said. "I want to talk to him." We didn't know this would be their last time together. He knew.

As Levi entered the room, I saw my dad's face light up. He gave Levi their secret handshake. He patted his bed and Levi carefully sat perched on the edge near his arm. My dad tenderly put his hand on Levi's hand and began talking to him.

He said, "Levi, I don't know who you're going to grow up to be, or what you're going to do in life, but I know it will be wonderful. I might not be here to see it, but I know you'll be someone really special. With your brilliant mind, you'll do great things!"

Levi smiled briefly and looked down at their hands with a bit of uncertainty.

My dad paused then, and in that pause, the conversation shifted. He waited for Levi to raise his head, gently locked eyes with him, and continued in a more serious, measured tone which was both loving and urgent. "I want you to remember one thing. In life, it comes down to this: *You've got to make the life you want. Be happy.*"

I was standing in the corner of the hospital room watching their exchange when my dad shared these words with my son. Physically, a strange, otherworldly feeling swept over me, from my head to my toes. Time seemed to stand still. I heard a muffled ringing in my ears like a cross between a low hum and the loudest cricket serenade from a midsummer night. I was frozen in place and felt as if the top of my head was going to blow off.

I knew I was witnessing one of those rare and pivotal moments, one that marked life before this moment, and life after.

I realize now that my dad effectively distilled his ninety-one years of life experience into one sentence that his thirteen-year-old grandson could hold onto as they faced the future apart.

But Levi wasn't the only one listening.

"Make the life you want. Be happy."

These words, meant to guide my son through a future without his grandfather, hit me like a grounding rod, a lightning bolt of truth, a powerful litmus test and a call for alignment.

"Make the life you want. Be happy."

He spoke a simple truth. There's no arguing with the logic here.

"Make the life you want. Be happy."

It's as easy and as difficult as that.

"Make the life you want. Be happy."

In this exact moment, my world shifted.

I loved my dad and knew he was speaking the truth. I believed in him and I believed in free will. Just as I believed in my son's ability to make choices that would result in a happy life, I had to believe in *my* ability to make a change in *my* life. I believed I could make the life I wanted. I believed I could finally be happy.

Suddenly, my life was in *my* control. Happiness was attainable. And making it happen was up to me.

"Make the life you want. Be happy."

This would become my battlecry, my mantra, my creed, my "why"!

My dad's words became the catalyst for me to connect to the experience of complete awareness and understanding that instantly calibrated me mentally, spiritually and physically with my own most basic truth and desire for what I wanted in my life. I stood in complete alignment. It was an instant recognition and understanding of a simple truth and a new way to live.

"Make the life you want. Be happy."

Any and all emotional debts were paid at this moment. His parting words of advice on how to live life in the most honest and authentic way have shaped my life since his death.

"Make the life you want. Be happy."

These words became my blueprint for life.

Your turn to find your "why".

"Make the life you want. Be happy."

An important aspect of beginning something like this is finding your own personal turning point and "why".

A turning point is an event that presents you with such intense clarification that you have no choice but to forge ahead in a new direction. It's a powerful landmark that marks the shift in how you did things before this event, and how you'll do them after.

What is your turning point?

_____

_____

_____

_____

_____

_____

_____

_____

_____

_____

Now find your "why". Take some time to think about what really resonates with you. You're looking for thoughts that will stick with you and make sense to you on both good days and bad days. This will be your mantra, the words that will always ring with powerful truth; the words that will serve as your beacon.

What is *your "why"*?

_____

_____

_____

_____

_____

_____

_____

_____

_____

_____

_____

_____

_____

CHAPTER 3

A Simple Pact: Nine Eat with Ease Commitments

Being so overweight was a true emotional and physical burden for me. The larger I got on the outside, the smaller I felt on the inside. I wanted, more than anything, for my physical body to reflect the kindness and beauty I felt on the inside. I was tired of missing out. Tired of being the "fat mom" in my kid's class. Tired of being in pain. Tired of not going places. Tired of automatically saying no, when I desperately wanted to say yes.

But finally, thanks to my dad, I had my "why"! *Make the life you want. Be happy.* I had a powerful truth inside me that was alive and wanted to be heard, and seen, and felt. I had a new mission. It was my beacon, and would guide me through the process of designing the life I wanted to live.

In order to create that aligned life, I knew I needed to lose weight—a lot of weight. I couldn't quit food like some sort of bad habit. I had to eat—I just needed to figure out how. I had no plan. But for the first time in my life, I had a deep desire to create a brand new reality for myself. I knew I was smart, massively empowered, and wanted to be successful. I felt driven to learn how to make this happen in a way that worked now, and would be sustainable for life.

It was time to start figuring this out.

I had no numeric goal. I didn't know exactly where I was going. But I would make the life I wanted. I would be happy.

I set myself up to be successful.

I made a simple pact that consisted of these nine commitments to myself:

Eat with Ease Commitment One:
Practice Patience

I commit to being patient and kind with myself in figuring this out.

Shifting from my childhood coping strategy of "time never stops," I realized that time was actually the most precious currency I had. With it, I could finally address my relationship with food by applying a practice of patience and self-kindness.

I didn't gain all that weight overnight. I wouldn't lose it overnight.

I trusted that I could effectively leverage the incredible gift of time to slowly make changes that reflected what I wanted.

Eat with Ease Commitment Two:
Be Curious

I commit to being curious!

When I patiently pondered how I might change my relationship with food, the old feelings of deprivation and failure arose. This time though, I didn't let them take control.

Instead, I thought about my mantra: *"Make the life you want. Be happy."* It felt a lot more powerful than the critical voice inside my head telling me I would fail. So, the first thing I did was allow myself to be curious.

I made no rash decisions. I didn't sign up for any programs. I didn't buy cases of shakes. I simply allowed myself to wonder about what felt right, what I could happily commit to doing, and what would eventually bring results.

I learned that curiosity is the state of wonder that leads to problem-solving. In being honest with myself, I realized that I didn't know how to proceed. It was hard to admit this to myself, but in acknowledging my state of not knowing, I was able to start gathering information.

I read everything I could get my hands on from trusted sources to learn about new foods and safe methods of exercise for larger bodies. I reflected on these new ideas and tried those that resonated with me, leaving behind those that didn't. I began to find joy in being curious, and in this process, I ultimately learned how to create a new relationship with food.

Eat with Ease Commitment Three:
End Punishment and Suffering around Food

I commit to ending food punishment and suffering.

In honor of each and every moment of food-related agony I endured throughout my lifetime of obesity, I declared an end to food punishment and suffering.

I suffered through a cycle of devastating food dysfunction for decades, so getting to the heart of this commitment took some figuring out. I realized that "not suffering" around food was both a mental and physical commitment to myself.

Mentally, I desperately needed to understand—and end—my unhealthy relationship with food. This included negative self-talk, feelings of deprivation and guilt, and using food as a coping mechanism.

Physically, I knew what I didn't want: There would be no fad diets. There would be no more yo-yoing. There would be no starving and nothing would taste awful. No foods would be restricted or considered "bad." There would be no retribution workouts. No plan would be unsustainable, and there would be no more failures. And most importantly, there would be no reason to give up.

To end my mental and physical punishment around food, I needed to get help.

Eat with Ease Commitment Four:
Find Expert Help

I commit to seeking help when needed.

Being curious helped me realize that I didn't know what I didn't know!

I had no idea how food worked in my body. I didn't know the difference between proteins, fats and carbohydrates, and that my body needed certain nutrients and macronutrients in order to function at its best. I had never even heard of my resting metabolic rate, let alone know how to work with it! So I met with a nutritionist, and over the course of several meetings, I learned about nutrition. I discovered my resting metabolic rate—how many calories *my* body needs to function at rest. I then learned which foods had which nutrients.

With these two pieces of information, my nutritionist next helped me decide what exercise I enjoyed and felt committed to. She then told me the daily number of calories my body requires in order to fuel myself, burn fat, have plenty of energy, support my growing muscles, and ultimately lose weight. This newfound knowledge enabled me to combine ingredients in ways that I loved which were also good for me! Understanding food guided me to create daily menus that were delicious, nutritious, and easy to follow. This made-for-me menu is a cornerstone of my success.

The work I did with my nutritionist led to a major weight-loss epiphany for me: *The secret to the body's ability to lose weight, which had eluded me for years, turned out to be a simple math problem.*

This is purely the physical side of weight loss. There are mental and spiritual aspects to this equation, too. (More on this in chapter six!) But physiologically speaking, losing weight involves knowing your own personal calculation: how *your* body functions and how it needs to move and be fueled in order to perform optimally.

I learned that the "magic" of a successful relationship with food is not found in an "eat this, don't eat that" approach. Rather, the key is in learning how your own body works, in order to create a sustainable strategy to eat foods you enjoy and move in ways that feel good. This optimizes your own unique physiology and wellness.

For every aspect of your physical and mental health, it is key to find a team of professionals who can personalize and support a customized plan that works for you.

Here are some examples of people to contact: dietician, nutritionist, therapist, coach, chiropractor, physical therapist, personal trainer, doctor, spiritual guide, meditation guru—do whatever you need to do, to learn what you need to know, in order to be successful!

Eat with Ease Commitment Five: Move My Body

I commit to moving my body every day.

I made a pact with myself that I would not place my head on the pillow unless I moved that day.

I got a pair of sneakers and went for a walk. I love music, so I created a super-fun playlist and listened to upbeat songs while I walked every day for an hour. This was fun and I looked forward to it!

Once I built up stamina with walking, I added other activities to keep myself interested in moving. I found a wonderful woman who was teaching Pilates in my neighborhood and I made an appointment to meet with her to see if Pilates was something I could do. She listened to me and my concerns: "Would I be able to do this in my large body? Would I break the equipment? Would I be able to keep up? Would I hurt myself?" She assessed my ability, listened to my trepidations, customized a plan, and worked with me, one session at a time, to help me gain strength and confidence. This was a game-changer for me. I not only found an exercise that was great for my body, but I also found a thoughtful teacher and friend.

It may take you a couple of visits to find a trainer who understands you and your needs. Don't give up! Once I found activities I enjoyed that I could actually do well, I realized that my body *required* movement. I felt stronger as I climbed stairs. I had a better state of mind in terms of stress relief, I slept great, and as I got stronger and more limber, the pain went away.

"But I'm Too Fat to Exercise!"

When I realized I needed to move, I was very out of shape. I had an old lower back injury, and didn't have good muscle tone. I was afraid that I would break the workout equipment. I was afraid that I would hurt myself. I had no confidence in my body's ability to heal and get strong. I believed that I was too fat to exercise.

Thankfully, I saw a chiropractor who helped me with my back when I was in acute pain. He was kind and recommended stretching and strengthening, and taught me stretches I could do at home. I shared my plan to lose weight and we discussed how I might safely exercise. In addition to stretching and walking, we talked about physical therapy. So, I got a prescription for physical therapy, and there I learned how to further stretch and strengthen my muscles. My physical therapist taught me how to properly use gym equipment. He stood right by my side when I used the treadmill. As my heart rate increased and I was still okay, I learned to step past my fear of moving. I learned I could trust my body. I started to physically heal.

To this day, I walk or do Pilates every day.

Eat with Ease Commitment Six:
Download and Use a Food and Exercise Tracker

I commit to diligently tracking my food and movement.

My body is a finely tuned machine and needs the best possible fuel along with some sort of activity. Once I met with the nutritionist, I realized that in order to be successful at weight loss, and to understand the caloric intake of different foods, I would have to track everything I ate, along with my daily exercise. This practice is a powerful tool! As I logged foods and moved, the number of calories adjusted, and I was, over time, able to create snacks and meals that both satisfied me *and* met my daily calorie and nutrient goal the nutritionist helped me establish.

"Oh, no! I have to log everything I eat? What a drag!" If this is the thought you're having right now about tracking your food and exercise, I would encourage you to rethink this! Treat your calorie counting app as a trusted accountant that's helping you work within a budget so that you can reach your goal *and* enjoy what you eat. It's a powerful tool. If you're running out of calories, this means you need to get creative about what you're eating so that you can be satisfied *and* well nourished. It's also fascinating to learn what effect exercise has on your body's metabolic system!

This is my most important tool for accountability and support. It helps me figure out how to eat delicious, satisfying meals, while I maintain my daily calorie and exercise goals.

Amy Freinberg-Trufas
Social Media Journal Entry

Resources are critical when undergoing a lifestyle change. I recommend having an arsenal of support at your disposal. This can include the advice of a nutritionist, a calorie intake app, an exercise plan, new recipes, friends who listen when you hit the wall, and your own internal compass.

One of my most important resources is using an app that calculates the number of calories I'm eating every day. I'm not selling or pushing anything here, other than good vibes (I hope), but I do want to encourage you to purchase a food and exercise app.

The one I'm using cost me $2.99, once. It shows me how I'm eating in terms of protein, carbohydrates, and fats, calculates the number of calories I'm eating, and the number of calories burned when I exercise. It also tracks my weight.

There are many apps out there that do similar things. Get one.

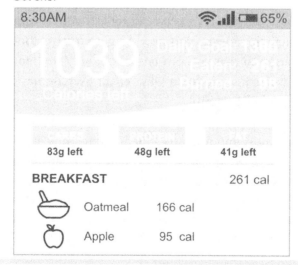

Eat with Ease Commitment Seven:
Discover My Love Tribe

I commit to finding a love tribe.

Along the way, I found people who both challenged and championed me! Having support in my mission to change my body and how I interacted with food was key to my success.

My love tribe consists of my nutritionist, my Pilates instructor, walking buddies, friends in real life and online, and even people who wave to me when they see me walking every day. These people may not be on your horizon right now, but believe me, they will appear along the way!

Eat with Ease Commitment Eight: Utilize New Tools

I commit to purchasing items that help me create healthy new habits:

In order to support my other commitments to myself in this new pact, I bought a few things that proved to be critical in my everyday routine:

 A smartphone food and exercise tracker to record nutrients and calories burned,

 A digital kitchen scale to help me develop a sense of portion size,

 A digital bathroom scale to weigh myself and track my progress,

 An air fryer with a wire rack and small cake pan to help me make delicious foods that I enjoy,

 A good pair of sneakers.

You may wish to buy these items plus whatever *you* need in order to ensure your own success.

Eat with Ease Commitment Nine: Write from the Spirit

I commit to keeping a journal.

At some point during my weight-loss journey, I started a private social media group and shared ideas and inspiration, recipes and challenges. I invited people from my love tribe to join me, as well as anyone who asked me, "What's your secret?" Know this: The process of losing weight is not a linear one. I had ups and downs. I had failures. I went off the rails a few times. But I always returned to my "why" and that one next right choice.

Being able to express these highs and lows (in either a private or public manner) proved to be therapeutic and useful! Whether poignant, humorous, or simply factual, each journal entry authentically documented my weight loss progress.

Amy Freinberg-Trufas
Social Media Journal Entry

Food is fuel, and like a luxury car, we need to put the very best fuel into our bodies to make them run well. This dawned on me while I was standing at a gas pump, putting premium gas in my car while mindlessly eating a bag of cheese puffs.

Also, like a luxury car, we need to run. Not literally, but we do need to exercise a minimum of five days a week. This can be walking, swimming, pilates, yoga, biking, dancing, online workouts, housework, gardening—whatever floats your boat. And don't think it has to be strenuous or hard on your body. It needn't be, and in fact, in my experience, gentle and steady is the way to go.

If you haven't already done so, download an app for your smartphone to help you start tracking what you eat and how much you exercise.

This all starts with one decision.

To start.

One step at a time, one foot in front of the other.

This is not a sprint, it's a marathon, a way of life.

Just start.

Your turn to commit.

"It was time to start figuring this out."

What commitments do you want to make to yourself?

_____

_____

_____

_____

_____

_____

_____

_____

_____

_____

_____

_____

_____

_____

_____

_____

CHAPTER 4

The Basics:
Six Eat with Ease
Discoveries

Just as having a large body made me feel small inside, the converse proved true: Eating well, exercising, and uncovering a healthier body made me feel expansive internally.

By saying "yes" to myself, I experienced an abundance of new thoughts, feelings, and ideas. These were epiphanies for me. Some of these revelatory ideas were small things, like how to enjoy take-out. Others were huge realizations about my own responses and behaviors that took me on journeys of self-reflection and discovery.

These breakthroughs altered how I perceived things, how I chose to act, and ultimately placed me on a trajectory for success.

At the beginning of my weight-loss journey, I reconceptu-alized "the basics." I thought about how to get started and how I might take that all-important first step, even though I had no idea where I was going. I experienced the power of one moment and one choice. I learned how success motivated me to keep going. And I completely rethought the notion of feeling "deprived" when it came to food. From there, I learned new coping skills which ultimately helped me recognize and interrupt my unhealthy food patterns.

These are the *Six Eat with Ease Discoveries!*

Eat with Ease Discovery One:
Getting Started

People ask me how I took that first step and what was different that made me ready to start this process. Once I discovered my "why", I was authentically aligned with my goal and positively motivated to make a change. This clarity brought limitless empowerment to my mind and will. I was exquisitely clear about *what* I wanted and needed to do.

I just didn't know *how* to do it.

So, I had to accept the fact that I had no idea how to lose weight. I had to be okay with not knowing. I had to trust myself. I had to allow myself the grace to be patient and curious about food and my body.

I had to trust a process that didn't yet exist.

If you are ready to take the first step, accept that you do not know everything you need to know right now. That's okay. Step anyway. All you need to get started is your "why".

Eat with Ease Discovery Two:
Harnessing the Power of the Next Right Choice

I had a seemingly insurmountable problem, one that, up to this point, had been impossible to overcome. I knew I couldn't fix it all at once. To solve it, I had to rethink it. So, I mentally broke my huge problem into pieces. I wondered about what I *could* do, and I realized that *I could commit to one simple choice.* Just one. In this thought, I realized that life is a succession of single moments and single choices. *In fact, everything* in life comes down to one moment and one choice.

This became my strategy: Just make the next "why-aligned" choice.

Amy Freinberg-Trufas
Social Media Journal Entry

Worrying, negative self-talk, not taking action—these are the things that lead to staying stuck. You might have to step out on a proverbial limb in order to believe this—but please accept for a moment that it's not too hard, not too big for you to solve, not out of your control, not hopeless, and not undoable. You may be feeling a great deal of discomfort. Know that this discomfort can help you facilitate life-altering change. Trust me for a moment. One moment, and entertain the idea that it is as easy as making the next right choice.

epiphany

We are all one choice away from a new life.

Eat with Ease Discovery Three:
The Cycle of Success

As the pounds started coming off, the feeling of success and how strong and able my body felt, for the first time in my life—was an inspiration to me. I saw the results of my agreement with myself and gained confidence. That newfound confidence motivated me to keep going.

And the entire cycle starts with one simple choice!

1.
Make One
Aligned Choice

4.
Feel Motivated
to Keep Going

Success

2.
See a
Positive Result

3.
Gain Confidence
in Your Ability
to Do This

———————— *epiphany* ————————

You are one success away from achieving your dream.

Eat with Ease Discovery Four:
Redefining Deprivation

When I thought about changing the way I ate, I thought I would have to give up "the good stuff." I worried that I wouldn't be able to eat what I wanted, when I wanted it. This didn't feel good.

I made a promise to myself that I would never suffer with food again. This included honoring my need to enjoy delicious foods in satisfying portions, so that I never felt hungry or deprived. Knowing that I needed this peace around food, I created recipes that met all of my requirements.

This promise ultimately created *food ease* for me.

 Amy Freinberg-Trufas
Social Media Journal Entry

We are all different and each and every one of us has a unique palate and level of fullness we need to reach in order to feel satisfied. Therefore, this is not about me telling you exactly what to eat. Instead, I suggest you begin to create or source food that meets all of your personal preferences; food that satisfies you in every way from taste to portion size. Your nutritionist or dietician can help you with this!

Once I had plenty of tasty food to eat that fit within my nutritional framework, the feelings of, "I guess I'll never be able to eat my favorite things again," were gone. And in order for this to work for me long term, they had to be.

Now, it's time to think about what deprivation *really* means.

Amy Freinberg-Trufas
Social Media Journal Entry

True Deprivation

I remember having an epiphany of sorts when I started this "lifestyle change" a couple of years back. Up to that time, I had always thought of dieting or healthy eating as depriving myself of something I wanted, needed and loved. I resented not being able to eat "what I wanted," so I half-heartedly lost a little weight, couldn't maintain it, and gained all the weight back—and then some.

But what dawned on me two years ago, and what has subsequently enabled and empowered me to begin, and even more importantly, maintain this lifestyle, was the realization that the true deprivation was happening when I was not feeding my body healthy foods, I was not exercising, I was saying "no" to experiences because of my weight, and I was not reflecting, on the outside, who I felt I truly was on the inside.

To me, and I mean this with as much conviction as I have in this world, **true deprivation is not being who you are meant to be in this world, right here and right now**.

If losing weight, "getting healthy," and caring for your body in a meaningful way would help express who you are, then stop depriving yourself of that!

Food is fuel. Make it high test, premium supreme, and run that engine like you mean it.

I eat plenty of delicious food now and I don't feel deprived. I feel empowered and well. I am energetic. I know this works and I can do this easily forever without any feelings of missing out whatsoever. The best part is I am doing this all within a body that reflects who I truly am.

In hindsight, here's a partial list of what I actually gave up:

~~*Negative self-talk*~~
~~*Self-abuse*~~
~~*Feeling stuck*~~
~~*Feeling scared*~~
~~*Food anxiety*~~
~~*Hopelessness*~~
~~*Feeling like a failure*~~
~~*Being disgusted with myself*~~
~~*Feeling out of control*~~

If you're reading this thinking, "That's great! But I have a robust habit of grabbing whatever I want to eat, whenever I want it, and I need to know what to do to break it. What else can I do when I have the urge to mindlessly eat?"

Beautiful! It's time to talk about coping.

Eat with Ease Discovery Five:
Coping—From Facing the Proverbial Fire Hose to Mastering
New Situations

What does the word "coping" mean to you? Does it feel like a negative word that makes you recall a stressful time when you struggled to deal with something difficult? As in, "I'm coping here the best I can!" Or, is it a positive feeling where you've met a challenge with a thoughtful plan and handled it brilliantly?

In my case, I used to feel like I was coping in the negative sense (things were coming at me faster than I could handle them, so I ate all the time) and now coping is synonymous with mastering. (I can deal with stress without automatically reaching for food.)

This was a process!

I had a series of epiphanies.

Up to this point, I hadn't *really* thought about food at all. Shocking, considering how much time I spent obsessing about it!

Food was my constant companion. Food was my emotional painkiller. Food was always "there for me," and I reached for it every time I had an uncomfortable emotion, craving or urge.

But here's the most ironic twist of all: I thought that reaching for food was easing my pain. It wasn't. My mindless interactions with food actually caused me a great deal of dis-ease. This was a sobering realization for me.

I was drowning in a cycle that was not serving me.

At the heart of my assignment with myself, I needed to take time to rethink what role food would play in my life.

If I didn't use food as an emotional anesthetic, how would I cope?

Eat with Ease Discovery Six:
How to Interrupt a Cycle No Longer Serving You

✓ Recognize

✓ Evaluate

✓ Interrupt

Recognize the Cycle

The first step in making a change is always recognition.

Amy Freinberg-Trufas
Social Media Journal Entry

When you realize that you're eating in response to a stressor, don't berate yourself! In fact, allow me to suggest that you congratulate yourself! You've discovered an opportunity to shift and effect huge change!

Evaluate the Cycle

Once I recognized that I was drowning in an unhealthy eating cycle, I was able to identify each of its elements and break the cycle down into small pieces:

Living through years of obesity,

I developed a **pattern**,

So that when a **situation** *arose,*

My **beliefs** *about myself,*

And how I had learned to **cope** *with stress,*

Resulted in an **action**,

And created a **behavior**,

And eventually a **habit**.

Pattern: The regular and repeated way in which something is done.

Situation: A set of circumstances in which one finds oneself.

Belief: Something one accepts as true or real, a firmly held opinion or conviction.

Cope: To deal with and attempt to overcome problems and difficulties.

Action: The physical manifestation of a choice, conscious or unconscious.

Behavior: The way in which a person acts in response to a particular situation or stimulus.

Habit: A settled or regular tendency or practice, especially one that is hard to give up.

Over time, I developed techniques to interrupt the cycle and create new actions.

Interrupt the Cycle

Looking at the elements of this cycle, I recognized that my default action when feeling stress was to reach for food. I needed to learn how to choose a new action. This is where I focused my attention in order to break the cycle of mindless eating.

Here's how I did this:

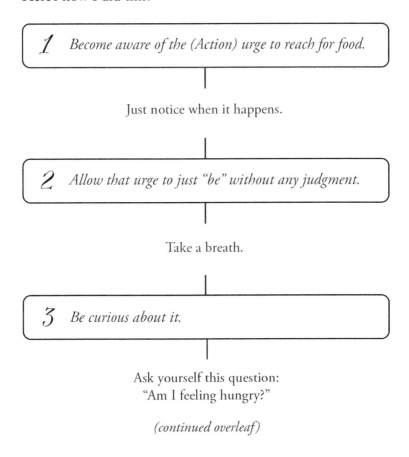

1 Become aware of the (Action) urge to reach for food.

Just notice when it happens.

2 Allow that urge to just "be" without any judgment.

Take a breath.

3 Be curious about it.

Ask yourself this question:
"Am I feeling hungry?"

(continued overleaf)

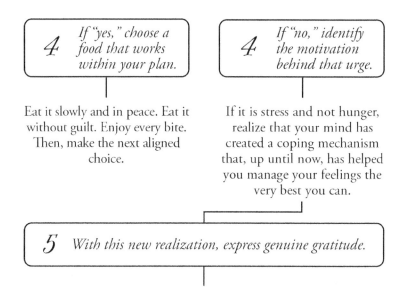

4 If "yes," choose a food that works within your plan.

4 If "no," identify the motivation behind that urge.

Eat it slowly and in peace. Eat it without guilt. Enjoy every bite. Then, make the next aligned choice.

If it is stress and not hunger, realize that your mind has created a coping mechanism that, up until now, has helped you manage your feelings the very best you can.

5 With this new realization, express genuine gratitude.

Internally thank all former versions of yourself that reached for food when stressed. Up until now, this response has helped you to survive.

When I do this, I imagine ten-year-old Amy feeling overwhelmed and reaching for food, and I thank her and surround her with love. Because she coped the best she could, I am here today to make a new choice.

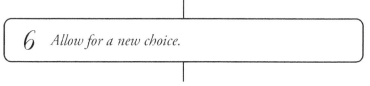

6 Allow for a new choice.

Take a few deep breaths. Drink some tea or water. Go for a walk. Read a book. Listen to music. Catch up with a friend.

7 Pat yourself on the back. You just made a new choice!

And a new choice disrupts this mindless cycle and eventually leads to a new habit.

Not a hard habit.

Just a new one.

This Is a Big Deal

When I intentionally chose my response to stress, and decided to take action in ways that aligned with my inner truth, I created powerful new habits and patterns. Over time and with practice, these new coping skills automatically activated when stressful feelings arose. This is how I moved the level of coping with stress from tolerating, to minimizing, to mastering!

Your turn to discover.

"We are all truly one choice away from a new life."

What is one new choice you can make today?

_____

_____

_____

_____

_____

_____

What are some coping skills you'd like to try instead of reaching for food?

_____

_____

_____

_____

_____

_____

Describe a cycle that's no longer serving you.

_____

_____

_____

_____

_____

How might you interrupt this cycle and create something new?

_____

_____

_____

_____

_____

What are you discovering about yourself?

_____

_____

_____

_____

_____

CHAPTER 5

Food:
Ten Eat with Ease
Strategies

I love to eat and have a true passion for food. Harnessing this passion to work *for me* instead of *against me* continues to be critical to my success.

Here are ten strategies I use to create that necessary balance between healthy eating (foods that fit within my daily goal) and enjoying delicious meals that make me feel completely satisfied.

Eat with Ease Strategy One:
Fill Up with Healthy Foods First

One technique that helped me in starting out, was to make sure I ate plenty of food that filled me up. Examples of these types of foods are oatmeal, a big salad full of fresh vegetables, some baby carrots, or a few cups of popcorn. In my mind, I crowded out the not-so-healthy foods I used to eat, with healthy foods that satisfied me.

Eat with Ease Strategy Two:
Discover What It Feels Like to Be Satisfied

I ate mindlessly for most of my life. When I realized that I didn't have to clean my plate, get second or third helpings of something that tasted good, or eat until I felt uncomfortably full, it was life-changing:

> It seems like every day, if I pay attention, I learn something that blows my mind. Here is today's mind-blower courtesy of my nutritionist: "Amy, you do know that you don't have to eat until you feel full or stuffed, right? Just eat until you don't feel hungry."

Eat with Ease Strategy Three:
Create Healthy Alternatives by Swapping Out Ingredients

A huge part of my ability to stick with my new plan was the flexibility to enjoy foods that I really loved to eat. I experimented until I found new ways to enjoy my favorite foods in moderation.

Amy Freinberg-Trufas
Social Media Journal Entry

Eating well and having a more healthy lifestyle doesn't have to mean deprivation for things we enjoy eating. Lately, I've been trying to alter recipes that I really enjoy (chocolate cake, muffins, cookies, baked goods) to create really good-tasting, healthy alternatives that are delicious and can be enjoyed in moderation. Items like Greek yogurt, applesauce, and banana can replace many fats in baked goods, and simply reducing the amount of sugar in a recipe results in a more healthy version of a cravable treat that satisfies. Let's face it. Sometimes we need a serious chocolate hit. Make it worth it!

Eat with Ease Strategy Four:
Dig In to a Dinner Salad That's Anything but Rabbit Food

I love a big salad! I customize them seasonally and include anything I'm craving.

My basic recipe for a delicious salad is:

Amy's Satisfying Salad

- A huge portion of interesting greens (spinach, spicy mix, herb mix, arugula, etc.),
- Seasonal vegetables, raw, roasted, or sauteed; chopped into bite-size pieces,
- Three ounces of lean protein (chicken, turkey, shrimp, beans, tofu),
- A tablespoon of chopped, toasted nuts,
- Chopped seasonal fresh or dried fruit (if using dried fruit, use about a tablespoon),
- A tablespoon of a strong cheese like feta, goat, or parmesan,
- Homemade vinaigrette—olive oil, lemon, balsamic vinegar, seasonings.

A wonderful way to get the flavor of the dressing on every bite and avoid making an otherwise healthy salad unhealthy, is to put the dressing in a small spray bottle! Just lightly mist your salad and dig in!

Eat with Ease Strategy Five:
Manage Late Night Snacking

I used to snack after dinner, mostly out of boredom. To combat this, I planned after dinner activities, like watching a movie, calling a friend, exercising, taking a walk, and even going to bed early with a good book. I found that if I didn't stay in the kitchen (my usual hang out), it was much easier to give up mindless snacking.

However, sometimes I was legitimately hungry, and did not want to blow my good eating for the day, nor trigger the cycle of feeling deprived, which historically led to raiding the snack drawer, then feeling like a failure.

I had to learn to manage those nighttime cravings. Here's what I came up with.

Amy Freinberg-Trufas
Social Media Journal Entry

Like my dad, I eat when I'm bored. I've been thinking about what I can eat at night that won't throw off all the healthy choices I've made throughout the day. Last night, I cut an apple into razor thin slices and sprinkled a little cinnamon on them. This was delicious and because there were so many pieces, it took me a while to eat them all!

Another before bed snack I love is three or four wheat crackers with a little dollop of lowfat cottage cheese on each. I've found that this snack really satisfies me with a tasty crunch, and the protein in the cottage cheese fills me up 'til morning.

I'm such a foodie! I look forward to going to bed. Sleep is the bridge to breakfast!

Eat with Ease Strategy Six:
Enjoy Restaurants and Take Out

There's no reason to deprive yourself of restaurant favorites! Here are some ways I partake in healthier versions of my favorite meals.

- ✓ When ordering a salad, I always request high-calorie top-pings (like nuts and cheese) and salad dressing to be served on the side. I ask for oil and vinegar (or fresh lemon) instead of high-calorie salad dressing. I skip any fried toppings. With these items on the side, I can add the salad toppings and dressings I want, and control added calories.

- ✓ Any side salad on the menu can be ordered as a dinner salad!

- ✓ Skip the bread basket. If it looks too good to pass up, I take one piece of bread and eat it mindfully. Rather than using butter, I dip it in a little dressing from my salad or in tomato sauce, if that's an option.

- ✓ Stay away from anything battered and fried. Instead, I opt for steamed, baked, or broiled, and ask them to prepare it without extra butter or oil. Often, fresh herbs and seasonings are enough!

- ✓ If I'm stumped about what to order, I ask the waitstaff for the healthiest thing on the menu, even if it means requesting that the chef create a custom meal featuring lots of seasonal vegetables and a favorite lean protein. I've asked for this several times, and I've been blown away by the delicious creations that are prepared for me!

- ✓ Skip the dessert. When I'm served dessert automatically, and it looks amazing, I take a bite or two, eat it slowly, savor it, and then I'm done with it. I have actually crumpled up a napkin and stuck it on top of a dessert that was rudely staring at me.

✓ If the meal was a treat, I don't take the leftovers home. If it was healthy and I can use the vegetables or lean protein as a meal or add it to a salad the next day, then I ask for a to-go box.

✓ To enjoy pizza from my favorite place, I order it with light cheese and no extra oil on top. (Many pizza chefs swirl cooking oil on top of the cheese right before it goes into the oven to make the cheese melt better.) Vegetable toppings are a good choice, and I always order a big salad with dressing on the side. I eat my salad first, and then I enjoy a delicious slice of pizza.

✓ Stay mindful of portion sizes. Restaurant portions have grown significantly and are often much larger than one serving size. I no longer feel compelled to clean my plate.

✓ I always use my food tracking app to plan ahead for special occasion meals, such as those at a restaurant, celebratory event, or holiday table. The morning of the event, I enter what I intend to eat all day, *before* I actually eat it, to see how different choices affect my daily goal. Using this method, I can plan ahead, maintain control, eat mindfully, and enjoy every special occasion, including special foods, without feeling the least bit guilty, deprived, or upset that I'm "off-track."

Amy Freinberg-Trufas
Social Media Journal Entry

It's a great night for some healthy Chinese food and my favorite dish is chicken with broccoli! I order it "steamed with sauce on the side." Delicious and super healthy!

Eat with Ease Strategy Seven:
Drink Plenty of Water

We have all heard how important it is to drink water, but I never knew why! Here are some things I learned from my nutritionist about the importance of hydration.

I learned that by the time we feel thirsty, our bodies are on their way to actually being dehydrated. Among other problems, dehydration decreases overall energy, both physical and mental. I learned that a good starting goal for drinking water is eight 8-ounce glasses per day. So, I created a new habit wherein I filled a gallon jug of purified, cool tap water in the morning, and left it on the counter at room temperature all day. My goal was to try to finish it. I eventually worked my way up to drinking most of it every day. In doing this, I found that I like room temperature water better than ice cold water because I found it easier to drink. I also noticed that drinking water throughout the day filled me up.

Eat with Ease Strategy Eight:
Don't Drink Your Calories

I learned that the calories I drink every day count the same as the food I eat!

For some reason, I didn't think liquid calories counted. When I started to track everything I ate and drank, I realized that I was hooked on diet cola and I sometimes drank three cans a day. My nutritionist shared that soda is an unhealthy beverage because it's bad for everything from my teeth, to creating inflammation in my body, to hidden caffeine content. She encouraged me to replace it. It was hard in the beginning, since I had a bona fide soda habit, so I decided to make sun tea using a gallon of water and a few herbal tea bags. Once it was brewed, the whole family enjoyed it!

Amy Freinberg-Trufas
Social Media Journal Entry

I realized that after I stopped eating and drinking things that had artificial ingredients in them, my tastes changed. In fact, I tried a sip of diet soda recently and could not stand it. Your tastes will change and you'll start craving the good stuff. Try it!

Eat with Ease Strategy Nine: Manage Cravings

Sometimes, I crave something that doesn't fit into my eating plan for the day.

A craving like this can take up tons of mental real estate. For example, let's say I want a brownie that would put me outside of my calorie goal for the day. I would think and think and think about that brownie and start to feel deprived. Then to distract myself, I might eat something "healthy," like a small handful of nuts. The whole time I'm thinking, "brownie, brownie, brownie . . ." Then I would eat some baby carrots. "Brownie, brownie, brownie." Then, maybe a small bowl of sweet cereal. By the time I ate all of these things that were distractions from the brownie that I *really* wanted, I ate more calories than the brownie itself! Plus, I deprived myself of something I really wanted—the brownie!

What developed over time for me, was to give myself a little time when I had a craving. I would drink a glass of water (because sometimes, I was just thirsty) or take a nice walk and listen to some music.

If I still wanted the brownie, I ate the brownie.

But, I made sure I enjoyed it. Every bite. And sometimes, I only wanted a bite or two! No matter how much I ate, though, guilt was not allowed. Punishment was not allowed. Retribution workout was not allowed.

Enjoy the heck out of whatever you are craving! Have the brownie. Love every bite. Stay present while you are eating it. Stop when you feel satisfied.

And simply make the next aligned choice.

Eat with Ease Strategy Ten:
Handle the Inevitable Stumble

You will stumble. You can handle it.

There were times I felt defeated. Once, I got sick and stopped tracking. I figured I knew everything I needed to know and could relax with my agreement with myself. I gained back twenty pounds over the next several months.

Then I forgave myself and simply made the next right choice.

> I'll admit it. I have been struggling for about a month now. I am not tracking consistently and finding reasons to skip exercise from time to time. I am not totally off-track, but I am not solidly on-track, either. I've gained three pounds, maybe five. No big deal, and I can get it back off, right? But only if I get back to my good habits. Having this under control is at the center of my feeling good about myself these days.

> I've been looking and looking for ways to get back on my path of what works for me. I know what it is. Tracking what I eat and exercising. Lately, I start off well in the morning, but I don't hold it together all day. I plan and it slips away.

"What's at the crux of this?" I ask myself. This morning, I watched an online lesson wherein the instructor suggested that we write ourselves a note, telling ourselves, our true inner selves, what we want for ourselves, and that we know and believe that we can get ourselves there. It's all based on love, everything is, so it has to be written by our highest self to ourselves when we need it most.

epiphany

When you stumble, remember that the answer isn't found by looking back. Instead, look ahead. You have a clean slate today, and in each and every moment.

Your turn to strategize.

What are you most passionate about, and how can it best serve you?

_____

_____

_____

_____

_____

_____

_____

What are some specific food strategies you can use in your everyday journey to eat with ease?

_____

_____

_____

_____

_____

_____

_____

CHAPTER 6

————

The Corsetry of Self-Love: An Eat with Ease Epiphany

I've discovered that I need to nurture my spirit just as I'm learning to nourish my body.

Growing up as I did, I experienced near-constant emotional pain. I suffered with what felt like a fatally wounded spirit. But now, things were different. As I started to lose weight, I realized that I was resilient. Not only was I still standing— I was still fighting. And in that fight, I realized that *I craved emotional ease.*

I desperately needed to let go of my painful past, and learn new ways to mentally and spiritually support myself, so that I could step freely into a happier, healthier life.

This undertaking felt both terrifying and necessary. I needed to compassionately and exhaustively explore the inner me in order to bridge my physical, emotional, and spiritual weight-loss experience. It required me to self-reflect, read, ask for help, get uncomfortable, and step, once again, into the unknown, with my hopeful heart that was hungry to heal.

Time to Reconnect with My Body

After decades of feeling disconnected from my body, I wanted to align my physical body with my inner self in healthy ways. I became interested in gentle, supported yoga. This was a safe way for me to stretch, gain body confidence, learn to breathe, and find calmness.

 Amy Freinberg-Trufas
Social Media Journal Entry

Everyone took science to some level in school. We learned that we are a collection of cells, all busy at work to maintain homeostasis in our bodies.

Yesterday during yoga, our instructor said, "We feed our bodies on the molecular level by what we eat, what we drink, and how we move and strengthen it. But don't forget—we also feed our cells with our own thoughts and messages within our bodies. So remember, your cells are listening to what you say internally."

Choose good food, plenty of water, plenty of movement that you enjoy, and speak nicely to yourself. All of these things are affecting each and every one of us on a molecular level.

Keep your building blocks strong.

In addition to yoga, I developed a daily walking habit which was key to my overall wellness. I found that I loved to take an hour-long walk, outside, in the fresh air and sunshine, while listening to my favorite music. This was a great stress reliever after a long day of work, too. And by walking every day, I honored my agreement with myself to move. This felt like a happy way to check that commitment off my daily list.

I am releasing my body weight with every step I take!

At bedtime, I listened to free guided meditations on my smartphone. Between moving my body every day, getting plenty of fresh air, and listening to nighttime meditations, I slept wonderfully.

Over time, these daily habits helped me discover a state of awareness in which I felt calm, connected, and present. This sense of ease fostered feelings of wellness and quiet confidence within me.

I finally felt like I was reflecting, on the outside, who I was on the inside! I was making the life I wanted. I felt happy. This was my goal—the holy grail of my weight-loss quest!

Little did I know that the biggest epiphany of all was yet to come.

I started this entire process in order to lose weight.

In hindsight, losing weight was actually the wonderful side effect of the new ways in which I interacted with myself. I had no idea that treating myself with kindness and respect throughout my weight-loss journey would lead to the most clarifying epiphany of all: Self-love.

Corsetry and Self-Love

My Pilates instructor taught me that exercise creates a physical corset for my body. Toned abdominal muscles protect the back and strengthen the core. With a stronger core, one can move about with more confidence and power, and even lift things safely.

Having a strong physical corset protects the body and reduces pain.

But what about the non-physical parts of me?

As I noticed my physical core getting stronger, I began to wonder: "Is it possible to create some sort of corset for my mind and spirit in order to strengthen my practices of patience, self-kindness, and even self-love?"

The answer? A resounding, "Yes!"

And in hindsight, this is exactly what I developed as a result of my weight-loss experience.

Here's how it unfolded:

I chose to be patient with myself. In this patience, I realized I needed to be curious about what might help me. I then sought the help of professional people who were kind and knowledgeable, and they gave me the tools I needed to be successful.

I kept things simple so that I wouldn't hit the wall and give up, since giving up was not an option.

I took steps which led to small successes that motivated me to keep going. When I screwed up, I remembered my "why" and simply made the next aligned choice.

Throughout this process, I began to understand who I was, how I thought, what I needed, and the dynamics behind my choices. I learned to take responsibility when appropriate, and to forgive myself and others, even if it meant bravely opening my fragile heart in order to heal, grow, and move forward.

I learned to recognize patterns that weren't serving me. I thanked my old, harmful responses for keeping all prior versions of me safe for as long as they did, and allowed myself to make new choices that felt aligned with my desire to create happiness for myself. This ultimately led to new patterns that fit my life well.

And throughout this entire process, with the many ups and downs, successes and failures, while sometimes feeling bewildered and beleaguered, vulnerable and hopeful, I did my best to practice kindness with myself—the same sort of kindness I would offer to a friend or loved one with a problem.

I gave myself that same space and time, thoughtfulness and love, patience, kindness, and encouragement. I believed that I was worth that allowance.

This practice created self-love.

I didn't know any of this when I started this process. And now, this practice has beautifully fashioned my physical, emotional and spiritual corsets.

Amy Freinberg-Trufas
Social Media Journal Entry

I have the sense, more increased than usual, that I should continue to challenge myself in terms of my comfort zone.

I was doing a tough online workout and the coach said, "It's normal to feel like you need to give up when you really push your body. That is simply the brain's way of keeping you comfortable." What? My brain will work against me to avoid pain and discomfort (physical and otherwise) just to try to maintain what is easy and familiar? Yes! My brain does this, by telling me to give up. "Being slim and healthy is not the real you, Amy, just go back to being fat."

Well, I have decided to start treating myself exactly the way I treat people around me, and that's with a great deal of respect, consideration, support, and kindness. I am going to continue to do the things that take me out of my comfort zone. Improv comedy group? Yes! Eating healthy foods and making sure I exercise every day? Yes! Believing that I am "worth it" in terms of effort, support, and outcome? Yes!

For me, my new comfort zone is being outside of what used to be my comfort zone. I cannot afford to go back to my old habits, nor do I want to.

Every day I wake up is a new opportunity to set things in motion as I see fit for my own happiness and life. So, whether that's choosing to fuel and move my body in a healthy way, or participating in things that bring forth my talents, or helping people with the amazing potential in their dreams, or even simply deciding to "try it again tomorrow," I am here and I am taking full advantage of this day....

Amy Freinberg-Trufas
Social Media Journal Entry

... When I experience the highs and lows of a lifestyle change like this, I am acutely aware of the love and support that's helped me to get here.

Thank you to each and every one of you for being on this journey with me.

Your turn to practice self-love.

"I've discovered that I need to nurture my spirit just as I'm learning to nourish my body."

What are three things you can do to reconnect with your body?

1. _____

2. _____

3. _____

What are three things you can do to nurture your spirit?

1. _____

2. _____

3. _____

Draw your spiritual corset.

CHAPTER 7

Honoring My Commitments: Maintaining Ease

It's a process. It's a process. It's a process. Change takes time.

I've easily lost a thousand pounds if you count every pound I've ever lost. But if you count each pound only once, from recorded highest to recorded lowest, I am 150 pounds lighter than my highest known weight.

Funny . . . I didn't know that once I lost all this weight, I'd have to continue on my plan to keep the weight off. I mistakenly believed that losing that much weight would miraculously reset my body's metabolism, and that I'd automatically be a carefree skinny person.

That didn't happen.

Weight loss is not a linear experience. Neither is maintaining weight loss.

Amy Freinberg-Trufas
Social Media Journal Entry

The New Wings Sometimes Don't Fly Right

I have something important to share: Basics and habits.

I've talked about forming habits before—for example, not letting my head hit the pillow unless I have exercised that day. But lately, I've learned that sticking with what works for each of us individually, "the basics," is critical to long term success.

This past winter was brutal. I didn't walk every day as was my habit. And I started to hear terms like "muscle confusion" and "tricking your metabolism." Friends who saw how I ate suggested that I needed more meat and protein. So, I started to change what I ate. I went to a new personal trainer who said I needed to really amp up my exercise, and since my body was more fit, I should do a lot more with it. I went to seven private gym sessions. I "pushed through" the knee pain I felt and reported to her. I did over one hundred lunges in one hour. I dutifully and resentfully went through the motions of being in a gym—on an elliptical and stair climber—all in the quest to raise my heart rate and confuse my metabolism.

Exercise, something I was learning to love, became a source of discomfort and I felt a huge sense of inadequacy.

I began to hate working out.

At the same time, I tried more protein and calories at the trainer's suggestion...

Amy Freinberg-Trufas
Social Media Journal Entry

...Summary of changes?
I strained my knee.
I gained eight pounds (and it wasn't muscle), and I
stopped exercising.

My chiropractor got my knee moving comfortably
and with some electrical stimulation, therapeutic
exercise, and careful movement, I should be fine.

I'm back to my basics now. Nothing complicated.
Eat good food.
Track what I eat.
Exercise daily.
Put myself on the list of things that are worthwhile.

I've lost five-and-a-half pounds.
I trust that I know what works for my body. And I
believe that you do, too.

Thank you so much for this friendship and support
here.

The new wings sometimes don't fly right.
So your support?
It means the world to me.

Little setbacks occur. Screw-ups happen. Life happens! Maybe
I don't feel well one day, and eat whatever I want and don't
track what I eat. No big deal. If I slip out of my new habit, as
soon as I realize it, I simply return to honoring my agreement
with myself and make the next right choice that best reflects
my "why".

And that next right choice opens the door to *ease*.

There's no reason to quit. There's no reason to circle the proverbial drain with erroneous thoughts of impending failure. It doesn't interest me to go back to eating poorly and being overweight. I know what that feels like. I was trapped in a body that didn't allow me to live. My old patterns will bring me back there.

I can do this journey again if I have to, but I don't need to experience that again. It's not easy to eat the way I used to. The food I used to enjoy doesn't taste good anymore, so I don't want it. I also can't eat the sheer volume I used to eat without feeling sick.

I have no need to burden myself emotionally or physically with extra weight.

And there's no reason to berate myself. Ever.

"Make the life you want. Be happy," is my central truth and anytime I start to waiver, I go back to this mantra.

It works for me for everything, every time.

Your turn to honor your commitments.

"The new wings sometimes don't fly right."

Setbacks happen. What are some strategies you can create to manage them?

_____

_____

_____

_____

_____

_____

_____

_____

_____

_____

_____

_____

_____

_____

CHAPTER 8

My Mom Finds Ease, I Find Ease

My Mom Finds Ease

At the end of her life, my mom was diagnosed with Alzheimer's disease.

Alzheimer's disease cruelly robbed my mom of her short-term memory. But it also mercifully dimmed her painful childhood, replete with her earliest memories of abandonment and abuse.

She was no longer masterful with words. She couldn't piece together coherent sentences, let alone create rhymes, poems or songs. Her gorgeous handwriting—beautifully executed strings of letters with pointed tips and perfectly formed bodies—faded away. There was no more sharp wit; no more sharp tongue.

She forgot how to cook.

She forgot that she had a history of agonizing emotions.

She forgot about alcohol.

But even in the deepest and cruelest recesses of Alzheimer's disease, she never forgot her children.

One evening, her loving caregiver expressed deep concern that my mom was seeing demons in her room. If Alzheimer's truly makes a person an exaggerated version of themselves as experts claim it does, imagine how tortured she was if her brain created demons.

Thankfully, this only happened once.

In Alzheimer's, my mom forgot her pain and she forgot her voids.

Alzheimer's finally quieted her demons.

She was at peace.

I Find Ease

When I sat down to write this book, I began the lengthy process of recounting and cataloging my memories. To my surprise, patterns emerged. Patterns that had gone unnoticed up to that point: Traumatic childhoods . . . Abandonment . . . Grandmothers raising grandchildren . . . Destructive addictions . . . Not knowing how to help someone in crisis . . . Poor coping skills . . . Suffering due to shame . . . Not taking responsibility . . . Not knowing how to forgive . . .

And pain . . . So much pain.

But for the first time in my life, I was witnessing these patterns as an adult, a mother, and a person who got to the other side of debilitating addiction.

In reflecting, I realized that because my mom was abandoned as a child, she didn't believe she was lovable. In this relentless agony, she ultimately abandoned herself, and felt forever lost. This devastating emotional fracture created that which my mom and I shared: A deep, painful void that we couldn't fill with anything external.

She tried to fill her void with alcohol, and sadly, never came to the understanding that what was missing in her life was self-esteem, self-worth and self-love.

Having felt exactly as she did for decades—unlovable, fractured, and lost—I understood completely. In that realization of what we shared, a seemingly unfillable, life-sucking hole, I felt only compassion for her.

I was, in fact, her.

In this realization, everything I thought and felt about my mom up to this point shattered: My lifelong fear of her was gone. My lack of respect for her was gone. My disgust for her was gone. My disappointment in her was gone. And all I felt for her was compassion.

And in that compassion, my only next feeling was forgiveness: Complete, loving, peaceful, freeing forgiveness.

For mom and for me.

I love you, mom.

Your turn to find ease.

What problematic relationship would you like to take a fresh look at from your current point of view?

_____

_____

_____

_____

_____

_____

_____

How can you reconceptualize this relationship to bring yourself a sense of ease?

_____

_____

_____

_____

_____

_____

_____

CHAPTER 9

Happy

"Make the life you want. Be happy."

Those words changed my life.

I sometimes think about my life before losing weight and I immediately remember feeling hopeless and out of control. I was in a constant state of angst and discomfort, wishing and hoping that I could somehow figure out how to lose weight. But most of all, I remember feeling like I just wasn't living.

I'm living now.

Several years have passed since I lost 150 pounds, and I continue to honor the simple pact I made with myself to remain purposeful with my thoughts and actions.

I abundantly practice patience, kindness and compassion with myself and others.

I continue to wonder and learn as I interact with myself and the world from a new body.

I say "yes!" a lot.

I embrace my passion for food and find joy in creating recipes that are both satisfying and delicious.

I ask for help from friends, guides, and mentors. These relationships are instrumental to my success.

I move every day. My body requires exercise and I love to be active.

I track everything I eat. I weigh myself every few days, and make adjustments to my habits as needed. This simple routine keeps me accountable, consistent, and aligned with my goals.

I write.

I lovingly tend to my physical, emotional, and spiritual corsets, taking care to embellish them with positive experiences and stitch them when they fray.

And I'm happy.

Every so often I still remind myself of my "why": "*Make the life you want. Be happy.*" But over the course of the past few years, it's become . . . me. I don't have to grab it with both hands and hold on for dear life.

It's forefront in my body, mind, and spirit.

"Make the life you want. Be happy."

It still works like a charm.

Your turn to be happy.

"Make the life you want. Be happy."

What are some ways you can increase the level of happiness in your life, now and in the future?

_____

_____

_____

_____

_____

_____

_____

_____

_____

_____

_____

_____

_____

_____

Your turn to have an epiphany.

Dear Reader,

Thank you for sharing in my journey.

My greatest wish is that you now create ease with anything that feels like it's not aligned with your deepest wishes for how you want to live.

To help you begin this process, I'd like to invite you to go back and look at all of the journal pages you've completed and assemble them.

Surprise!

You've created your own guide to making the life you want.

Congratulations!

xo

Amy

CHAPTER 10

_____

Ease

Ease

I wondered.
And where there was confusion, there is order.
What was unconsciousness is now mindful.
Where there was ignorance, there is knowing,
And where there was fear, there is safety.

I created.
And where there was scarcity, there is abundance.
What felt hopeless now holds promise.
Where there was hunger, there is contentment,
And where there was disgust, there is kindness.

I grew.
And where there was frailty, there is power.
What felt stressful now provides peace.
Where there was no, there is yes!
And where there was shame, there is forgiveness.

I loved.
And where there was dis-ease, there is ease.
What felt irrelevant now offers purpose.
Where there was sadness, there is love.
And where I was lost, I found myself.

I live.

What I Wish Doctors Knew about Being Fat

First, do no harm.

I lost faith in doctors.

Upon graduating medical school, doctors take the Hippocratic Oath, an ethical standard which among other things, espouses: "First, do no harm." This means that above all else, their first job is to cause no additional harm or suffering to the person seeking their expertise.

As a fat person, my interactions with doctors and nurses were historically callous at best and traumatizing at worst. I only went to the doctor's office when I was really sick and even then, I avoided getting on the scale. For an overweight person who needs an antibiotic for something as simple as a sinus infection, the fear of a disdain-filled admonishment about my weight from a doctor or nurse who clearly didn't understand the breadth of my problems was very real. So much so, that I didn't seek medical attention when I needed it.

First, do no harm.

I was harmed time and time again by doctors and ancillary medical personnel who didn't know how to identify the range of problems I suffered with. Nor did they take the time to ask. Instead, they assumed they knew who they were dealing with by my appearance and let their biases and false narratives about overweight people cloud their professional judgement.

I remember a particularly upsetting appointment with a new, slim, insensitive female doctor who said, "You're morbidly obese. *Morbidly*. That means death. Look at me! Even sitting here, I don't sit still. I shake my leg and wiggle. Do what I do! Jiggle your legs when you sit. Move constantly. Stay active. Your laziness isn't helping you." At that time, I was going to college full-time and working four part-time jobs. Laziness was not my problem.

First, do no harm.

When my family doctor sent me home on Halloween when he could have handed me an apple and told me how great my costume was, he harmed me. When the German weight-loss doctor didn't supply me with an examination gown that covered my eleven-year-old body—in a weight loss clinic—and then rebuked me for my bright sense of humor, she harmed me. When the nurses at fat camp decided it was acceptable to have us line up, strip naked, get weighed and broadcast our weight to a room full of people, they harmed me. When the slim, female doctor assumed that because I was fat, I was lazy, she harmed me.

First, do no harm.

Not once did any of my medical providers ask me if I was safe at home, or if I was open to—or even interested in—having a conversation about how I may begin the process of losing weight.

The medical community has much to learn about how to best serve people who are struggling with extra weight, and their unique physical, emotional, spiritual and societal needs. Their inability to connect, communicate, check their biases, and understand the individual sitting in front of them, leaves an entire population of people underserved.

This problem is rampant in the medical community. And it's time they do better.

First, do no harm.

Made in United States
North Haven, CT
17 March 2022

17253673R00096